Corporate Restructuring Through Disinvestment

(An Indian Perspective)

Corporate Restructuring Through Disinvestment

(An Indian Perspective)

Harjit Singh
MFC (Gold Medalist), MBA (Dual), M.Phil. (Com.), Ph.D. (Com.)
Associate Professor,
Institute of Marketing and Management
New Delhi-110016

PUBLISHING FOR ONE WORLD

NEW AGE INTERNATIONAL (P) LIMITED, PUBLISHERS
(formerly Wiley Eastern Limited)
New Delhi • Bangalore • Chennai • Cochin • Guwahati • Hyderabad
Jalandhar • Kolkata • Lucknow • Mumbai • Ranchi
Visit us at **www.newagepublishers.com**

Published by New Age International (P) Ltd., Publishers
First Edition: 2007

ISBN 13 : 978-81-224-2162-0

ISBN 10 : 81-224-2162-8

Rs. 125.00

C-07-06-1641

Printed in India at Nisha Enterprises, Delhi.
Typeset at In-house, Delhi.

PUBLISHING FOR ONE WORLD

NEW AGE INTERNATIONAL (P) LIMITED, PUBLISHERS
(formerly Wiley Eastern Limited)
4835/24, Ansari Road, Daryaganj, New Delhi - 110002
Visit us at **www.newagepublishers.com**

PREFACE

Public sector undertakings in India were viewed as a mechanism for structural transformation of the economy and for growth with equity and social justice. They were established to attain the 'commanding heights' of the economy of the country and achieve rapid growth of industrialization and economic development. There has been phenomenal and tremendous growth of PSE's in India. But some of these public sector units later became 'white elephant' and started incurring losses. Several of them became chronically sick industries. This alarmed the entire corporate to gear up to the expectation of the market. Open competition erupted and threat to the traditional business houses was witnessed.

Many business houses collapsed and a lot of engineering activities came into being for the survival of business. Corporate restructuring is one such area, which has emerged recently. It is an umbrella term that includes mergers and consolidations, disinvestment and liquidations, and various types of battles for corporate restructuring can and has been used to mean almost any change in operations, capital structure and ownership that is not part of the firm's ordinary course of business.

Disinvestment is not a vehicle to bridge budgetary gaps but is an integral part of corporate restructuring which itself should be viewed as part of re-equipping Indian industry to become globally competitive. This book in its present form is an icy shower in the hinterland of disinvestment and is intended to provide a comprehensive text to cover this much talked but less understood issue in the Indian perspective and is essential reading for anyone who wants to know the nuts and bolts of disinvestment, its present status and interested in knowing how it is gaining worldwide acceptance.

The book is divided into seven chapters. Chapter 1 explains what Corporate Restructuring is all about and sets the tone for disinvestment. Chapter 2 deals with public sector's objectives, background of public ownership, evolution of public sector policy in India and the need for disinvesting PSEs. Chapter 3 analyses in detail the disinvestment drive in India, the concept of disinvestment, year-wise disinvestment of PSEs and contribution of disinvestment proceeds in meeting fiscal deficit. Chapter 4 is all about privatization framework.

Chapter 5 deals with theoretical perspective on the effects of ownership and competition on efficiency of public sector enterprises and based on the empirical evidence, measures the performance of these PSEs. Changes and Impacts on Industry Structure and Operations find place in chapter 6. Finally the chapter 7 besides suggestions and recommendations, discusses the various inferences drawn from previous chapters and presents the summary and conclusion part.

Though primarily targeted for post-graduate students, Corporate Restructuring Through Disinvestment should be useful to the practicing managers, researchers and all serious students of a critical economic reform process.

I will appreciate and greatfully acknowledge the suggestions and comments from the readers and fellow teachers of the subject.

DR. HARJIT SINGH

ACKNOWLEDGEMENT

"Practice makes a man perfect" is a legendary aphorism and when a person gets guidance of experts of the respective field, the knowledge gained is invaluable. In the light of the foregoing, I offer my deep sense of gratitude to Dr. S.D. Vashishtha, Professor and Head, Department of Commerce, M.D. University, Rohtak who has been a continuous source of inspiration in carrying out this book.

This trifle work of mine would have been a zygote, if not have achieved the support, cooperation and blessings of few people, without whom, I would not have been able to materialize my book. Therefore, I would like to put my heartfelt thank to Dr. Jagjit Singh, Senior Professor and Executive President, Institute of Marketing and Management (IMM), Delhi, for their guidance, support and continuous encouragement while writing this book.

I would like to acknowledge the scholastic hand provided by Dr. Sanjay Jain of Delhi School of Economics, University of Delhi, Prof. Vinay Dutta, Fore School of Management, New Delhi, Prof. R. Vinayak, Prof. S.S. Chahal, and Prof. M.S. Malik from M.D. University, Rohtak and Prof. K.K. Uppal of Punjabi University, Chandigarh.

I am also grateful to executives of various public enterprises, librarians and staff members of various libraries visited by me during the preparation of book, for extending their helping hand and providing relevant information and data, whenever required by me.

It would not be fair on my part if I forget to express my thanks to all the staff members of Department of Commerce, M.D. University, Rohtak and Institute of Marketing and Management, New Delhi for their worthy guidance and support.

Genetics and inheritance matter as much as anything so vital so important. I respect my inheritance; I am grateful to my beloved parents and my brother-in-law Mr. Sabby Sachdev, Ph.D. candidate, Virginia, USA who deserve, nothing short of honour. I thank them for their love, affection and sincere hand for assisting me and creating an ambience where I could put my best into this book.

I am also indebted to my wife Prabhjot Kaur, Ministry of Defence and my father-in-law Mr. K.S. Sachdeva, Ministry of Home Affairs for having provided enormous support and encouragement inspite of bearing the brunt of elongated study hours which encroached upon the time normally meant for meeting my family obligations.

Friends are nature's gifts, and I'm gifted with lot of friends who have gone to extremes to support my actions, my deeds and helped me in various ways for successful completion of this book. My indebtness to other works has been duly acknowledged at the relevant places.

I would also like to thank people at infinity for helping me in any way they could.

Dr. Harjit Singh

LIST OF ABBREVIATIONS

ADR	American Depository Receipt
ASI	Annual Survey of Industries
ASSOCHAM	The Associated Chambers of Commerce & Industry of India.
AY	Andrew Yule and Company Limited
BALCO	Bharat Aluminium Company Limited
BEL	Bharat Electronics Limited
BEML	Bharat Earth Movers Limited
BHEL	Bharat Heavy Electricals Limited
BIFR	Board for Industrial and Financial Reconstruction
BRPL	Bongaigaon Refinery and Petrochemicals Limited
BSE	Bombay Stock Exchange
CAPM	Capital Asset Pricing Model
C & AG	Comptroller and Auditor General of India
CCD	Cabinet Committee on Disinvestment
CEL	Central Electronics Limited
CII	Confederation of Indian Industry
CIS	Commonwealth of Independent States
CMD	Chairman and Managing Director
CMIE	Centre for Monitoring the Indian Economy
CONCOR	Container Corporation of India Limited
CPI	Consumer Price Index
CRL	Cochin Refineries Limited
DCF	Discounted Cash Flow
DCI	Dredging Corporation of India Limited
DMCCL	Dharamsi Morarji Chemical Company Limited
DOT	Department of Telecommunications
DPE	Department of Public Enterprises
EIL	Engineers India Limited
EPIL	Engineering Projects (India) Limited
ESOP	Employees Stock Option
ET & T	Electronics Trade and Technology Development Corporation Limited

FACT	Fertilizers and Chemicals (Travancore) Limited
FDI	Foreign Direct Investments
FERA	Foreign Exchange Regulation Act
FICCI	Federation of Indian Chambers of Commerce & Industry
FIIs	Foreign Institutional Investors
FY	Financial Year
GAAP	Generally Accepted Accounting Principles
GATT	General Agreement on Trade & Tariff
GAIL	Gas Authority of India Limited
GDP	Gross Domestic Product
GDR	Global Depository Receipt
GSL	Goa Shipyard Limited
HAL	Hindustan Aeronautics Limited
HCIL	Hotel Corporation of India Limited
HCL	Hindustan Cables Limited
HIL	Hindustan Insecticides Limited
HINDALCO	Hindustan Aluminium Company
HLL	Hindustan Latex Limited
HMT	Hindustan Machine Tools Limited
HOCL	Hindustan Organic Chemicals Limited
HPCL	Hindustan Petroleum Corporation Limited
HPF	Hindustan Photo Films Manufacturing Corporation Limited
HPL	Hindustan Prefab Limited
HSCL	Hindustan Steel Works Construction Limited
HTL	Hindustan Teleprinters Limited
HVOC	Hindustan Vegetable Oils Corporation Limited
HZL	Hindustan Zinc Limited
ICRA	Investment Information & Credit Rating Agency
IDBI	Industrial Development Bank of India
IDPL	Indian Drugs & Pharmaceuticals Ltd.
IFFCO	Indian Farmers Fertilizers Cooperative
IISCO	Indian Iron and Steel Company Limited
IMF	International Monetary Fund
IMG	Inter-Ministerial Group
IOC	Indian Oil Corporation Limited
IPCL	Indian Petrochemicals Corporation Limited
IPO	Initial Public Offering
IRCON	Indian Railway Construction Company Limited
ITDC	India Tourism Development Corporation Limited
KIOCL	Kudremukh Iron Ore Company Limited

L & T	Larsen & Toubro
LMBO	Leveraged Management Bye-Out
LPG	Liquified Petroleum Gas
LSE	London Stock Exchange
MBO	Management Bye-Out
MECL	Mineral Exploration Corporation Limited
MECON	Metallurgical & Engineering Consultants (India) Limited
MFIL	Modern Food Industries (India) Limited
MFL	Madras Fertilizers Limited
MNCs	Multinational Companies
MOIL	Manganese Ore (India) Limited
MoU	Memorandum of Understanding
MPP	Mass Privatization Programme
MRL	Madras Refineries Limited
MRTP	Monopoly and Restrictive Trade Practices
MTNL	Mahanagar Telephone Nigam Limited
NALCO	National Aluminium Company Limited
NAV	Net Asset Value
NCAER	National Council of Applied Economic Research
NFL	National Fertilizers Limited
NHPC	National Hydro-electric Power Corporation Limited
NI	Net Income
NIF	National Investment Funds
NIP	New Industrial Policy
NLC	Neyveli Lignite Corporation Limited
NMDC	National Mineral Development Corporation Limited
NRI	Non Resident Indian
NSE	National Stock Exchange
NSSO	National Sample Survey Organisation
NTPC	National Thermal Power Corporation Limited
NTT	Nippon Telegraph and Telephone
ONGC	Oil and Natural Gas Corporation Limited
OPEC	Organisation of Petroleum Exporting Countries
PAT	Profit After Tax
PBDIT	Profit Before Depreciation, Interest and Tax
PEC	Projects and Equipments Corporation Limited
PECV	Profit Earning Capacity Value
PER	Price Earning Ratio
PES	Public Enterprises Survey
PHL	Pawan Hans Helicopters Limited
PIB	Press Information Bureau
PIM	Preliminary Information Memorandum

POWER	Power Grid Corporation of India Limited
PPCL	Pyrites, Phosphates and Chemicals Limited
PPE	Power Plant Equipment
PPL	Paradeep Phosphates Limited
PSEs	Public Sector Enterprises
R & D	Research and Development
RCFL	Rashtriya Chemicals and Fertilizers Limited
RICL	Rehabilitation Industries Corporation Limited
RITES	Rail India Technical and Economic Services Limited
ROA	Return on Assets
ROCE	Return on Capital Employed
ROE	Return on Equity
ROS	Return on Sales
RPS	Retention Pricing Scheme
SAIL	Steel Authority of India Limited
SCI	Shipping Corporation of India Limited
SDF	Steel Development Fund
SEBI	Securities and Exchange Board of India
SIL	Sponge Iron India Limited
SLPE	State Level Public Enterprises
SOEs	State Owned Enterprises
STC	State Trading Corporation of India Limited
SWOT	Strengths, Weaknesses, Opportunities and Threats
TFP	Total Factor Productivity
TISCO	Tata Iron and Steel Company
UK	United Kingdom
USA	United States of America
USD	US Dollars
UTI	Unit Trust of India
VRS	Voluntary Retirement Scheme
VSNL	Videsh Sanchar Nigam Limited
WACC	Weighted Average Cost of Capital
WTO	World Trade Organisation

List of Tables

LIST OF GRAPHS

CONTENTS

CHAPTER 1

Corporate Restructuring: An Introduction

Introduction

There has been phenomenal and tremendous growth of Public Sector Enterprises (PSEs) in India. The four decades until 1991 witnessed a substantial growth and expansion of the public sector and were viewed as a mechanism for structural transformation of the economy and for growth with equity and social justice. These were created as private initiative was not forthcoming in vital sectors of the economy. Eventually, the perception that public sector should acquire the commanding heights of the economy led to government involvement in diverse areas of economic activity, many of which could have been performed by the private sector. The public sector thus lost its original status and strategic focus, which shifted to supply of goods and services on subsidized rates and creation of employment. This led to inefficiencies, neglect of resource mobilization for modernization, increased dependence on unproductive borrowings, lack of motivation to improve efficiency and increase in fiscal deficit of the Central and State Governments.

The situation became worsen with the public sector undertakings having political appointees as Chairpersons regardless of their functional contributions and capabilities. This was compounded by the short tenure appointments of service-officers as Managing Directors leading to lack of continuity, professionalism and accountability. Above all, the judicial ruling that public sector enterprises are an instrument of the state as defined in Article -12 of the Constitution placed them at a disadvantage compared to the private sector units in the matter of functional and financial autonomy. There are, therefore, inherent problems in the case of PSEs, which do not allow these to function strictly on commercial considerations, because of fear of Comptroller and Auditor General of India (CAG's) criticism, and even criminal processes through Central Bureau of Investigation (CBI) and Central Vigilance Commission (CVC) and consequent lack of boldness in decision-making. India, having one-fourth population below poverty line, had to provide safety net to targeted population through multi-level and multi-user charges. The performance of PSEs, however, was far from satisfactory. As a result, the industrial policy heralded the economic liberalization substantially contracted the role of the public sector. The number of industries reserved for the public sector has been reduced to eight and in 2001 May, all industries except atomic energy and railway transport were thrown open to the private sector. Corporate restructuring by way of disinvestment is now an important aspect of the new policy. In short, the industrial development of the country is now left mostly to the private sector.

Further, intense competition, rapid technological changes, major corporate accounting scandals, and rising stock market volatility have increased the burden on managers to deliver superior performance and value for their shareholders. In the modern 'winner takes all' economy, companies that fail to meet this challenge will face the certain loss of their independence, if not extinction. Corporate restructuring has enabled thousands of organizations around the world to respond more quickly and effectively to new opportunities and unexpected pressures, thereby reestablishing their competitive advantage. It has an equally profound impact on the many more thousands of suppliers, customers, and competitors that do business with restructured firms.

Background Leading to Corporate Restructuring Decisions

The last two decades have witnessed a dramatic increase in various forms of corporate restructuring, particularly in the western economies. Takeovers, divestitures, management buyouts (MBOs), going private transactions and bankruptcies have all played a significant role in restructuring firms during the economic downturn of the early 1980s to the boom period of the mid-1980s and 1990s. Like almost every country, India too welcomed Liberalization, Privatization and Globalization (LPG) as a development paradigm. Therefore, for nearly a decade since the onset of economic liberalization in India, a key component—disinvestment/privatization—

remained dormant. The usual explanation has been that unstable governments could not overcome the many vested interests, from rent seeking bureaucrats and ministers to public sector trade unions. Further, complex economic environment in which market forces are changing quickly and radically and competition is becoming ever fiercer, corporate risk is on the rise. Public sector had lost much of its former efficiency. Their costs were rising even financial performance results were embarrassed. Sales promotion efforts were mostly wasted. Marketing function had poor response. Rate of new product failure was alarming. This alarmed the entire corporate to gear up to the expectation of the market. Open competition erupted and threat to the traditional business houses was witnessed.

Many business houses collapsed and a lot of reengineering activities came into being for the survival to save Indian corporate sector. Corporate restructuring is one such area, which has emerged recently. It is an umbrella term that includes mergers, acquisitions, consolidations, disinvestment and liquidations, and various types of battles for corporate restructuring can and has been used to mean almost any change in operations, capital structure and ownership that is not part of the firm's ordinary course of business.

For this purpose, a number of official committees under direct supervision of Government of India and members of parliament have examined various aspects of public sector performance and emphasized the need for better incentives and greater autonomy & accountability for the management of the Public Sector Enterprises (PSEs). Thus, restructuring of equity by way of disinvestment is the key determinant of the public sector reforms and the policy over the last two decades. Almost all countries whether developing or developed have engaged in substantial programme of restructuring the equity (ownership) pattern by selling public sector enterprises. The common perception behind such restructuring the Indian public corporate is that these programmes are highly triumphant and hence desirable.

Corporate Restructuring: Meaning and Definition

Corporate restructuring provides the necessary objectivity and methodical support to bring a company back on the road to success. It involves making radical changes in the composition of the businesses in the company's portfolio. This type of corporate action is usually made when there are significant problems in a company, which are causing some form of financial harm and putting the overall business in jeopardy. The hope is that through restructuring, a company can eliminate financial harm and improve the business. Corporate restructuring is defined by Hoskisson and Turk (1990) as a major change in the composition of a firm's assets combined with a major change in its corporate strategy. It usually involves selling off (or liquidating) businesses in large diversified (M-Form) firms, either voluntarily through spin-offs or involuntarily through hostile takeovers. Restructuring also can occur once a leveraged buyout (LBO) of a firm has been completed. Thus, from Hoskisson and Turk (1990) point of view, corporate restructuring, in turn, is likely to:

(a) result in the correction of inadequate governance patterns,
(b) create a more focused diversification strategy,
(c) increase strategic control,
(d) reduce reliance on bureaucratic control through reduced corporate staff, and
(e) increase the performance of the firm and shareholder wealth.

According to Tiwari (2001), corporate restructuring means the series of process to restructure asset structure, financial structure, and corporate governance, helping the survival and the growth of a corporation. Although the extent of corporate restructuring includes a distressed company as a target in a narrow term, it includes an inefficient company as a target in a broader term.

Generally speaking, any restructuring of the liability and stockholders equity components of a financial balance sheet is normally undertaken because the issuer does not generate enough cash flow to service its debt and other liabilities. Restructuring may include deferral of principal or interest payments on debt, disinvestment of equity shares, equalization of debt or other liabilities, and, in bankruptcy, modification or termination of burdensome contractual commitments. The expectation is that through restructuring, a company can eliminate financial harm and improve the business. Characteristics of corporate restructuring can include:

- Any major public relation campaign to reposition the company with consumers.
- Changes in corporate management functioning.
- Disinvesting the shares and utilise the sum received in the areas of extreme importance.
- Shifting of operations such as manufacturing to lower-cost locations.
- Outsourcing of some basic operations such as payroll and technical support to a more efficient third party.
- Refinancing of corporate debt to reduce interest payments.
- Renegotiation of labour contracts to reduce overhead.

- Reorganization of functions such as marketing, sales, and distribution.
- Sale of underutilized/abandoned assets, such as patents, brands and composition secrets.

Therefore, when a company is having trouble making payments on its debt, it will often consolidate and adjust the terms of the debt in a debt restructuring. After a debt restructuring, the payments on debt are more manageable for the company and the likelihood of payment to bondholders increases. A company restructures its operations or structure by cutting costs, such as payroll, or reducing its size through the sale of assets. This is often seen as necessary when the current situation at a company is one that may lead to its collapse.

Types of Restructuring

1. Portfolio restructuring

Portfolio restructuring means making additions to or disposals from companies' businesses *e.g.*, through acquisitions or spin-offs and is normally applicable to derivative products. In simple terms, it is decomposition of a portfolio's asset mix by selling off undesired asset types (equities, debt, or cash) or specific securities within that class, while simultaneously buying desired types or securities. For this, often a company is asked to bid on an old portfolio and give an offering of the desired portfolio.

When to use portfolio restructuring strategy?

Corporate experience throughout the globe reveals that there is as such no clear-cut time horizon when portfolio restructuring becomes essential for a nation. But some shortcomings when persist indicate the need for thinking portfolio restructuring. These are as follows:

- Core business divisions fall upon hard times.
- Long-term performance prospects are unpleasant.
- 'Wave of the future' technologies or products appear and major shake-up is required to build position in a potentially big new industry.
- 'Unique opportunity' emerges and some existing business units must be sold to finance new acquisition.
- Major businesses in portfolio become unappealing and unproductive.

The areas of improvement include:

- Enhanced return on the value of the portfolio.
- Making radical changes in mix and percentage make-up of types of businesses in portfolio via both divestitures and new acquisitions.
- Overall decrease in total reinvestment needs.

2. Financial restructuring

It is changing the capital structure of an organisation *e.g.*, through leveraged buy-outs etc. for the purpose of bringing out a company from financial difficulty.

Essentials of financial restructuring

The purpose of financial restructuring is not achieved if following points are not considered:

- Creating greater levels of control in your internal auditing and reporting processes.
- Developing a more efficient means of meeting company's debt obligations and manage cash more successfully.
- Exploring the possibility of debt-equity exchange (wherein existing debt is exchanged for new equity shares, transforming creditors into equity holders).
- To find ways to maintain customer loyalty and generate recurring revenues as part of a long-term growth strategy.
- To identify new, or underutilized, assets that can boost company's bottom line.
- To reconfigure company's entire pay, benefits and retirement provisions to create greater financial efficiencies.
- Further, audit department should adjust its risk management techniques to reflect today's online realities, and set-up itself as a valuable management resource resulting in increased cash flow yields.

3. Organizational restructuring

In the fast changing world, organizational restructuring is essential to stay up to date. Managers periodically examine the organizational structure of their company to assure that it maintains to provide an environment for organizational development. Organizations that cannot or don't learn become obsolete. The reasons why organizations should restructure themselves are:

- Actions of global competitors, work force values, demands, and diversity.

- Individual development and transition.
- New and fast expanding markets.
- Regulatory, political and ethical constraints from the environment.
- To innovate men, materials, machines, technology, work culture, and organizational structure.

These are few reasons for organizational restructuring. However, organizational restructuring in these situations should only follow once the business strategy has been changed—for the very same reasons.

Essentials of organizational restructuring

- Accountability for results.
- Assessment of gaps (if any) in existing roles which make any structural changes effective.
- Clear communication and role clarity.
- Development and execution of an organizational change management plan to address and define the drivers of any structural change, as well as the impact on the business of the change options.
- Employees cooperation.
- Management commitment to a new business strategy to address the changes in market, technology, regulations, etc.
- Organization's sense of purpose, vision and commitment towards change.
- Positive human behaviour and improving performance, further requires changing behaviour.
- Proper assessment of impact of internal and external factors causing change on the business strategy.
- Proper understanding of cost of organizational change.

When to use organizational restructuring?

- Complaints of subjective and biased performance appraisals are coming regularly.
- Employees' morale is deteriorating.
- Increase in employees turnover.
- Organizational communications gap is increasing and deteriorating day by day resulting in clash between different levels of management.
- Overall work force productivity is deteriorating despite continuous efforts.
- Parts of the organization are significantly over or under staffed.
- Present skills and capabilities are inefficient to meet current or expected operational requirements.

- Regular conflicts regarding accountability for results.
- Technology and/or innovation are creating changes in work flow and production processes.

The Role of Government in Times of Crisis: Foreign Experience

Corporate restructuring at country level/large level is potentially one of the most difficult tasks faced by country and inter country economic policymakers. The need for such kind of large-scale restructuring arises in the aftermath of a country financial crisis when corporate distress is omnipresent. The thriving completion of restructuring requires a government to take the lead in establishing restructuring priorities, tackling market failures, reforming the political, legal and tax systems, and, perhaps most important, dealing with obstacles posed by commanding interest groups.

The confront of corporate restructuring

Country/large-scale corporate restructuring made necessary by a financial crisis is one of the most intimidating challenges faced by economic policymakers. The government is forced to take a leading role, even if indirectly, because of the need to prioritize policy goals, address market failures, reform the political, legal and tax systems, and deal with the resistance of commanding interest groups. The objectives of such large-scale corporate restructuring are in essence to restructure viable corporations and liquidate nonviable ones, restore the health of the financial sector, and create the conditions for long-term economic survival. It has been observed that successful government-led corporate restructuring policies generally follow a set sequence. *First,* the government formulates macroeconomic and legal policies that lay the foundation for thriving restructuring. *Then,* financial restructuring must start to institute the proper incentives for banks to take a responsibility in restructuring and get credit curving again. Only then can corporate restructuring begin in earnest with the separating out of the viable from nonviable organisations—restructuring the former and liquidating the latter.

The major government-led corporate restructuring tools are mergers, acquisitions, mediation, takeover, incentive schemes, bank recapitalization, and the appointment of directors to lead the restructuring. Once the government has achieved its desired goals, the government must reduce its intervention in support of restructuring drive.

Laying the foundation of restructuring

The prime aim of a country reforms is to maximize shareholders' returns. Sometimes, to achieve that, nations need to undergo corporate restructuring. Corporate restructuring on a large-scale is usually made necessary by a systemic financial crisis—defined as a severe disruption of financial markets that, by impairing their ability to function, has large and adverse effects on the economy of a nation. The intertwining of the corporate and financial sectors that defines a systemic crisis requires that the restructuring should address both sectors simultaneously. But successful restructuring is not possible without a strong foundation set-up by government action across the gamut of economic policies. For this, first of all, whole economic stability must be well-established to provide the assurance needed for debt restructuring. Stable prices, interest rates, and exchange rates are needed for creditors, debtors, and potential investors to have enough certainty to accomplish business. Further, the size and nature of corporate distress must be quickly assessed by the authorities, banks, and advisers to determine if the problems are systemic and thus whether the government should take a leading role.

Essentials of country level restructuring

For restructuring to be successful at country level, a supportive regulatory, legal, and accounting environment is necessary. Important legal aspects of restructuring include foreclosure standards, foreign investment rules, and merger, acquisition and business combinations policies. Further, regulations prevailing debt-equity conversions and asset sales frequently need to be changed to make possible novel and complex restructuring transactions.

Secondly, corporate governance must be brought up to inter country standards to provide incentives for viable firms to restructure their balance sheets and maximize their value. Improved governance is needed not only to push managers to restructure the existing debt stock, but also to operate profitably and improve future profit flows.

Restructuring the financial sector

Corporate restructuring cannot commence even if the foundation has been laid without restructuring the financial sector. The draining of bank capital as part of the crisis will usually lead to a sharp curtail in lending to viable and nonviable corporations alike, worsening the overall reduction. Moreover, banks must have the capital and incentives to play a role in restructuring. The very first task of financial restructuring is to separate out the viable from the nonviable financial institutions to the extent possible.

To do this work, financing and technical assistance from inter country financial organizations can be helpful, as in Indonesia following the 1997 crisis.

The appropriate strategy is that nonviable banks should be taken over by the government and their assets eventually sold or shifted to an asset management company, while viable banks should be recapitalized. Banks should be directly recapitalized for normal operation or else, in the absence of strong competitive pressures; they may impede recovery by recapitalizing themselves indirectly through wide interest rate spreads. At the same time the government should ensure that bank regulation and supervision is strong enough to maintain a stable banking sector.

The degree of circularity here is that the separation of viable banks from nonviable banks is helped by completion of the same task for corporations, which itself is aided by financial restructuring. The best way to close this circle seems to be rapid restructuring of the banks because a cutback in bank financing to corporations amplifies the overall contraction, and has irreversible consequences—such as the sale of assets too cheaply.

Restructuring the corporate sector

Mark R. Stone (2002) advices that corporate restructuring can commence in earnest only when banks and market players are willing and able to participate. As with the financial sector, the first task is distinguishing viable from nonviable[1] organizations. The conclusion of nonviable firms ensures that they do not absorb credit or worsen bank losses. However, the identification of nonviable corporations is complicated by the poor overall performance of the corporate sector during and just after the crisis. Viable and nonviable firms can be identified using profit simulations and balance sheet projections, as well as best judgment.

Liquidating nonviable corporations during a systemic crisis usually requires the establishment of new liquidation mechanisms that avoid standard court-based bankruptcy procedures. In this regard, the bankruptcy code of the United States can be taken as the standard minimal government involvement approach. In practice, however, this code has a strong liquidation bias—some 90 per cent of cases end in liquidation, and reorganization takes a long time. Moreover, courts are usually unable to handle a large volume of cases, lack expertise, and may be subject to the influence of vested interests.

[1] Nonviable organizations are those whose liquidation value is greater than their value as a going concern, taking into account potential restructuring costs, the 'equilibrium' exchange rate, and interest rates.

Giving debtors protection from bankruptcy during mediation proceedings allows corporations that are later judged to be viable to remain operating and enables the orderly liquidation of nonviable corporations. If debtors are protected from bankruptcy, however, monitoring of the corporations is needed to ensure that incumbent managers do not hive off the most profitable assets. Liquidation can be speeded up by special courts or new bankruptcy laws. Hungary introduced a tough bankruptcy law in 1991 under which firms in arrears were required to submit reorganization plans to creditors; if agreement was not reached, firms were liquidated. Also, a standstill on payments to banks during negotiations allows cash-strapped corporations to continue operation while their viability is being decided. Without effective bankruptcy procedures, restructuring can be significantly slowed down, as happened in many of the transition countries, in Mexico in 1995, and especially in Indonesia after the 1997 Asian crisis.

The government must also decide on disposal of the assets of liquidated corporations. Delays in asset disposal tie up economic resources, slow economic recovery, and impede corporate restructuring. Of course, the balance sheets of viable corporations must be restructured. Restructuring will involve private domestic and foreign creditors, newly state-owned creditors, and asset management corporations, as well as stakeholders such as unions and governments. Usually, balance sheet restructuring takes place through the reduction of debt or through the conversion of debt into equity. Often minority creditors slow debt restructuring by threatening to liquidate the debtor in an attempt to force majority creditors to buy them out on favourable terms. This coordination problem can be avoided by the rules that allow less-than-unanimous creditor approval of reorganization plans, which can be enforced by government moral suasion, by prior creditor agreement to a set of principles, or through bankruptcy proceedings.

Early completion of relatively clear-cut transactions can jump-start the restructuring program. Restructuring is often delayed by difficulties in valuing transactions because of economic instability and unreliable corporate data. Long delays in implementing bankruptcy reforms greatly slowed the large-scale corporate restructuring efforts of the mid- and late 1990s. By early 2000, Mexico had still not completed bankruptcy law reform, even though there had been a sharp drop in bank claims on the private sector since the country's 1995 crisis. In East Asia, ineffectual bankruptcy laws stymied corporate restructuring by allowing nonviable firms to stay afloat, which not only precluded banks from collecting the underlying collateral, but also acted as a disincentive for viable firms to repay their debt—further hurting the banks. Delays in bankruptcy reform are due mainly to pressures from groups and individuals who would be hurt by the liquidation of nonviable firms, as well as by the time needed to bring up to speed legal systems faced with a sudden increase in bankruptcy cases.

Transparency is essential for bankruptcy reform: regular government disclosure of all the aspects of restructuring can make clear the obstacles put in the way by vested interest groups, and thus lead to public pressure to accelerate reform[2].

Some common lessons regarding large-scale corporate restructuring that can be drawn from the experience of countries like Chile, Mexico, Poland, Thailand and Malaysia are as follows:

- Top management should be prepared to take on a large role as soon as a crisis is judged to be systemic.
- A sound supporting macroeconomic and legal environment is essential.
- Measures should be taken quickly to offset the social costs of crisis and restructuring.
- Restructuring should be based on a holistic and transparent strategy encompassing corporate and financial restructuring.
- Restructuring goals should be stated at the outset, and sunset provisions embedded into the enabling legislation for new restructuring institutions based on these goals.
- A determined effort to establish effective bankruptcy procedures in the face of pressures from vested interest groups is essential.
- Large-scale post-crisis corporate restructuring takes a minimum of one to three years to complete, on average.
- Finally, crisis can ultimately boost long-term growth prospects both by weakening special interests that had previously blocked change, and through the successful completion of corporate restructuring.

Evolution in India

Business combinations, corporate restructuring, financial reengineering, corporate reorganizations are the terms used for restructuring the corporate sector. But in India, corporate restructuring by way of disinvestment of public sector enterprises has become a fashionable concept in recent years. Management experts have written volumes on disinvestment, privitisation, and downsizing the public corporations and the individual and a whole host of other issues ranging from compensation systems to strategic

[2] Mark, R. Stone (2002), Corporate Sector Restructuring: The Role of Government in Times of Crisis, Economic Issue No. 31, available online on IMF website.

acquisitions for market entry opportunities. One of the concerns is about the global competition.

Compelled by the present economic scenario and market trends, corporate restructuring through mergers, amalgamations, takeovers and acquisitions, has emerged as the best form of survival and growth. The opening up of the Indian economy and the government's decision to disinvest has made corporate restructuring more relevant today.

In the last few years, India has followed the worldwide trends in restructuring amongst companies through disinvestment. Companies are being taken over, units are being hived off, sold for equity, and joint ventures tantamount to acquisitions are being made and so on. It may be reasonably being stated that the quantum of disinvestment, mergers and acquisitions in the last few years must be more than the corresponding quantum in the four and a half decades post independence.

One issue which is still unanswered is that whether PSEs' restructuring should be done prior to disinvestment or after disinvestment by the private management. Experience suggests that a healthy and competitive PSE can fetch better price in the market in comparison to a sick PSE. But then the question arises about the suitability of further putting money in sick PSEs, and the capability and the competence of the present management to undertake the restructuring, which they had done before. While a restructured PSE would most likely fetch better price in the market, one should make a cost-benefit analysis to find out the extent of incremental social and financial benefit the Government would receive by selling the restructured units. However, the experience in the market has shown that at the pre-disinvestment stage, Government should undertake organizational, financial and labour restructuring to enhance the value of the unit and leave the business restructuring to the strategic buyer who should decide what to drop and what to retain depending upon the objective of this strategic purchase. It appears to be unlikely that restructuring of the PSEs' would be undertaken properly timely, and boldly. In fact, the Government will have to take active interest and take quick decision in this regard. With the present Government system and bureaucracy as it is, the objective of effective restructuring may not be possible. Therefore, there is a need for constituting a professionally oriented agency such as Public Enterprises Restructuring Authority. Understanding the need, the Government may enact a special act through Parliament. This Authority should be vested with sufficient power for taking policy, financial, technical decision etc.

Effects of Corporate Restructuring

What kind of influence does corporate restructuring have on a firm's real value-added, labour productivity, employment pattern and salary?, are as follows:

EMPLOYMENT PATTERN: Companies are moving away from relying on workers on open-ended, full-time contracts and, increasingly, use part-time, temporary, contingent and contract workers. Hire and fire policy has become the fashion of corporate sector.

JOB OPPORTUNITY: New jobs are coming up and the content of jobs is being expanded to encompass a greater variety of tasks. Working hours are round the clock. Opportunities are now a mouse click away.

ORGANIZATION: There is a trend towards flatter organizational structures. It is clear that corporate restructuring is a deep and pervasive phenomenon across the globe. The increasing trend of mergers and acquisitions is one of the clearest and most readily measurable manifestations of restructuring.

PLACE OF WORK: Thanks to Information and Communication Technology (ICT) revolution, online methods of doing business, E-commerce, and tele-working, have become popular.

SALARY: Salary is no bar for deserving. Profit-sharing and various types of bonuses are becoming common and salary is linked with performance.

SKILLS: New working methods are raising skill levels and requirements, and work force thus is required to continuously upgrade their skills so as to be able to cope with the changing corporate demand.

WORKING TIME: Increases in demand are met by overtime work or by "a more flexible approach as to when and how to work", so as to extend operating hours without having to pay overtime rates. 24×7, night shifts, odd timings, and pick and drop facilities are talked about these days.

Corporate Restructuring and NPL Disposition

Corporate restructuring is similar to distressed debt disposition (commonly popular as NPL disposition) with respect to its relationship with distressed debt, but it has a basic difference. Whereas distressed debt disposition refers to carving out distressed debt, a kind of distressed asset from financial institution, corporate restructuring means restructuring the corporate itself and is often seen as necessary when the current situation at a company is one that may lead to its collapse.

Downsizing, mergers and restructuring are a reality of today's business environment. As protectionist trade barriers have fallen, European organizations have been increasingly required to reposition themselves to meet the challenges of the global market place. In the home market, deregulation, increased competition as well as technological changes have required organizations to become more efficient and effective. As a result of these market pressures, it is inevitable that organizations analyze and redesign all aspects of their business to remain competitive.

As part of this process, organizations are downsizing at an unprecedented scale, and merger, acquisition and disinvestment activity remains high. Although there may be benefits to downsizing or mergers on paper, they are not easily translated into understanding or acceptance in the human dimension where once loyal employees must come to terms with being unemployed.

Summary

The present economy of India is passing through a process of crucial transformation. For the last four decades we have been following a path in which the public sector was expected to be the engine of growth. However, from the middle of the seventies, disappointment with the public sector had started, but the voices of protest were very weak and periodic. But the continuous failure of public sector to fulfill the role assigned to it intensified the voices of protest. The opening of certain sectors earlier reserved for public sector was undertaken in the beginning of eighties but the government was to some extent hesitant to make a clear statement. Then ultimately in the year 1991, under the stewardship of Dr. Manmohan Singh, then finance minister, the process of corporate restructuring through disinvestment was actually started and got momentum. The decisions of opening up of public sector for private players, incentives to foreign direct investment, removal of licensing policy, removed restrictions on investment and expansion, access to foreign technology and mergers and acquisitions by Indian giants in and outside the country ushered in a process of economic reforms in India.

The corporate restructuring, often compared to medical surgery, is a process of treatment for ailing companies based on the professional diagnosis. It is the act of partially dismantling and reorganizing a company for the purpose of making it more efficient and 'therefore' more profitable. It generally involves selling off portions of the company and making severe staff reductions. It is often done as part of a bankruptcy or of a takeover by another firm, particularly a leveraged buyout by a private equity firm. It may also be done by a new CEO hired specifically to make the difficult and controversial decisions required to save or reposition the company. The selling of shares of the company, such as a division that is no longer profitable or which has distracted management from its core business, can greatly improve the company's financial performance. Staff reductions are often accomplished partly through the selling or closing of unprofitable portions of the company and partly by consolidating or outsourcing parts of the company that perform redundant functions (such as payroll, human resources, and training) leftover from old acquisitions that were never fully integrated into the parent organization. This is often seen as necessary when the current situation at a company is one that may lead to collapse.

Just as the goal of medical surgery lies in the recovery of a patient, the aim of a corporate restructuring is the rehabilitation of a distressed company. As the patient needs a hospital to be recovered, the ailing company requires a restructuring vehicle to be rehabilitated. In all, the corporate restructuring has become a more sophisticated and more dynamic environment in which to operate. Whilst it is good to remind ourselves how far we have come, we are also aware that there is plenty more room for growth and let us hope that the next couple of years, which will be very important from an economic perspective, continue to provide more scope for the rescue and turnaround of faltering businesses in India.

REFERENCES

1. KIM, H.T. *A Study on Junk Bond Market in Korea,* Research Paper 99-03, Korea Securities Research Institute, March, 1999.
2. KIM, H.T. and LEE, H.J. *The Corporate Restructuring Market in Korea: Frontier in Capital Market,* Research Paper 01–01, Korea Securities Research Institute, 2001.
3. MORGAN STANLEY DEAN WITTER. *Distressed Asset Markets in Asia,* June 2000.

CHAPTER 2

Public Sector in India

Introduction

Public sector has been considered as one of the major instruments of state intervention activity in the development process of an economy. The Public Sector Enterprises alias PSEs, which were once considered as engine of economic growth of the country, are today, at the beginning of the new millennium, no more regarded as such. Rather, these PSEs are now termed as 'Means of earning money', 'Centres of poor performance', 'Hub of frauds and corruption', 'Ports of no growth', 'Bureaucrats' toy', etc. Even the recently earned laurels like *Navaratna*[1] and *Mini-Navaratna*[2] by some of the surplus making PSEs under Administered Pricing System got a jerk by a very simple word called 'disinvestment'. They were supposed to attain the 'commanding heights' of the economy of the country and achieve rapid growth of industrialization and economic development. But some of these PSEs later became 'white elephant' and started incurring losses. Several of them became chronically sick industries. Then it was felt by the Central Government that PSEs have outlived the purposes for which they were once created and it is not a wise decision to block huge public fund in the PSEs which are symbols of sickness, inefficiency and stagnation—'a drain on the public exchequer'. Moreover, when disinvestment is the fad of the day, private sector should be given a role to play in modelling the behavioural pattern of a PSE also. It is, as such, necessary to withdraw huge money blocked up in public sectors and to invest in the other parts of economy where private sector is not ready to invest and are of public importance like primary education, public health and social insurance etc.

Public Sector: Meaning and Definition

Public sector is that part of economic and administrative life that deals with the delivery of goods and services by and for the government, whether national, regional or local/municipal. In short, a public sector is "an enterprise where there is no private ownership, where its functions are not merely confined to the maximization of profits or the promotion of the private interest of the enterprise, but are governed by the public or social interest, and where the management is responsible to the government either directly as in a department undertaking or indirectly as in government companies and corporations."

Objectives

One of the basic objectives of setting up the public sector in India was to build infrastructure for economic development and rapid economic growth. The public sector which was promoted as an instrument for implementation of the government's socio-economic policies had a multitude of objectives set for them. The main objectives for setting up public sectors are:

- To help in rapid economic growth and industrialisation of the country and put it on the industrial map of the world.
- To promote balanced regional development.
- To create employment opportunities.
- To promote redistribution of income and wealth.
- To assist small-scale and ancillary industries.

Background of Public Ownership

Main reasons for the public ownership of industries could be as under:

1. The development of public enterprises was seen as an appropriate policy response to bring about improvements in the economy, both in the developed as well as the developing countries. There appeared to be an economic consensus around the world accepting public enterprises as an inevitable part of the economy, especially to manage natural monopolies and the core industry. While the public sector contributed significantly to the development effort, the low rates of return on such investments and the inability of governments to finance the growing demands of such industries

changed the consensus in favour of economic liberalization and privatization from the 1970s in almost all countries.

2. Such industries could not have been developed by private sector during 1940s or 1950s as there was not enough money in the money market and also entrepreneurship was limited. So the government used high rates of taxation and deficit inflationary financing to develop public industries.
3. *Rescue missions (Nationalization):* Sometimes the government had to step in to rescue certain enterprises, whose closure could result in significant loss of jobs and also due to several other economic and social reasons.
4. *Control of strategic sectors:* Another rationale for state ownership was the belief that the investment in states and control of the strategic sectors of the economy was necessary for the economic development of these sectors and security of the country.
5. *Developing the economy:* A few PSEs were established to balance or replace weak private sectors, to develop the industrially backward areas, to generate employment and to make goods available at lower cost.

Evolution of Public Sector Policy in India

- In the 1948 Industrial Policy Resolution, the manufacture of arms and ammunition, production and control of atomic energy, ownership and management of railways became the state monopoly. Six fundamental industries *viz.*, iron & steel, coal, aircraft manufacturing, ship building, mineral oils, manufacturing of telephone, telegraph and wireless apparatus were to be developed by the state. All other areas were left open to private initiatives.
- Within a decade of laying down the policy parameters in 1948, another policy statement was issued in April 1956 by the Government to give a new orientation to the 'mixed economy' concept. This Policy Resolution categorized industries into three groups:

  (i) Industries exclusively reserved for development by the state *viz.*, arms and ammunition; iron & steel, heavy castings & forging, heavy plant & machinery required for iron and steel production and mining; heavy electrical plant, coal and lignite, zinc, copper, lead, aircraft, ship building and telecommunication equipments.

  (ii) Industries, which would progressively be state owned and in which the state will generally take the initiative in establishing new undertakings but in which private enterprise will also be expected to supplement the efforts of the state. These include aluminum, fertilizers, other minerals, machine tools, ferro-alloys and tools, basic and intermediate products required by chemical industries, antibiotics and other essential drugs, synthetic rubber, carbonization of coal, chemical pulp, road and sea transport.

(iii) The remaining industries were left open for the private sector initiatives.

- In the context of significant changes in fiscal, monetary, trade and industrial policies, the need for review of continued presence of the public sector in a wide range of activity was felt in the nineties. A new strategy for the public sector was spelt out in the policy statement in July 1991, which marked a turning point in the policy guidelines as far as the public sector was concerned. The philosophy behind the New Economic Policy was that the state should, by and large leave industry and commerce to the private sector and concentrate on those areas where it had a special or unique responsibility.

The broad features of 1991 reforms were:

A. Portfolio of public sector investment would be reviewed with a view to focus the public sector on strategic, high-tech and essential infrastructure, whereas some reservation for the public sector was being retained. There would be no bar for areas of exclusivity to be opened up to the private sector selectively. Similarly, the public sector would also be allowed entry in areas not reserved for it.

B. The list of industries reserved for public sector was reduced from seventeen included in the Industrial Policy Resolution of 1956 to only eight in the July 1991 Policy Statement; subsequently, in March 1993, two more items were dereserved. The six industries for exclusive operation in public sector were:

(i) Arms and ammunition and the allied items of defence equipment, defence aircrafts and warships;

(ii) Atomic energy;

(iii) Coal and lignite;

(iv) Mineral oils;

(v) Minerals specified in the schedule to Atomic Energy (Control of Production and Use) Order 1953; and

(vi) Railway transport.

Other developments since then were:

1. Dereservation of mining activity and with this coal extraction has been permitted for captive use by user industries.
2. Invitations have been extended to private sector to invest in oil exploration and refining, otherwise reserved for public sector, as well as infrastructure projects like roads, ports, telecom etc.
3. Private sector venture in power generation even with 100% foreign equity has also been allowed.

The Need for Disinvestment

Since inception, public sector enterprises have played an important role in achieving the objective of economic growth with social justice. However, economic compulsions, *viz.*, deterioration of balance of payment position and increasing fiscal deficit led to adoption of a new approach towards the public sector in 1991. Disinvestment of public sector undertakings (PSEs) is one of the policy measures adopted by the Government of India for providing financial discipline and improve the performance of this sector in tune with the new economic policy of Liberalisation, Privatisation and Globalisation, (LPG) through the 1991 Industrial Policy Statement. The aims of disinvestments policy were:

- Global perception that the private ownership leads to better use of resources and their more efficient allocation. Throughout the world, the preference for market economy received a boost after it was realized that the state could no longer meet the growing demands of the economy and the state shareholding inevitably had to come down. The 'State in business' argument thus lost out and also the presumption that direct and comprehensive control over the economic life of citizens from the central government can deliver results better than those of a more liberal system that directly responds according to the market driven forces.
- Another reason for adoption of disinvestment policies around the globe has been the inability of the governments to raise high taxes, pursue deficit/inflationary financing and the development of money markets and private entrepreneurship.
- Further, technology and World Trade Organization (WTO) commitments have made the world a global village and unless industries, including public industries do not quickly restructure, they would not be able to survive. Public enterprises, because of the nature of their ownership, can restructure slowly and hence the logic of privatization gets stronger. Besides, techniques are now

available to control public monopolies like Power and Telecom, where consumer interests can be better protected by regulation/ competition, and investment of public money to ensure protection of consumer interests is no longer a convincing argument. The objectives of the disinvestment drive vary from improving efficiency of the PSEs to transformation of the society.

The primary objectives for disinvesting the PSEs

- Releasing the large amount of public resources locked up in non-strategic PSEs, for re-deployment in areas that are much higher on social priority, such as public health, family welfare, primary education and social and essential infrastructure.
- Stemming further outflow of these scarce public resources for sustaining the unviable non-strategic PSEs.
- Reducing the public debt that is threatening to assume unmanageable proportions.
- Transferring the commercial risk to which the tax-payers' money locked up in the public sector is exposed to the private sector wherever the private sector is willing and able to step-in—the money that is deployed in the PSEs is truly the public money, and is exposed to an entirely avoidable and needless risk in most cases.
- Releasing other tangible and intangible resources, such as large manpower, currently locked up in managing the PSEs, and their time and energy, for re-deployment in areas that are much higher on the social priority but are short of such resources.

The other benefits expected to be derived from disinvestment are:

- Disinvestment would also facilitate in freeing the PSEs from the government control and introduction of corporate governance in the privatized companies resulting in wider distribution of wealth through offering of shares of privatized companies to small investors and employees.
- Disinvestment would expose the privatized companies to market discipline, thereby forcing them to respond to the market forces much faster and cater to their business needs in a more professional manner.
- Disinvestment would have a beneficial effect on the capital market—increase in floating stock would give the market more depth and liquidity, give investors easier exit options, help in

establishing more accurate benchmarks for valuation and pricing, and facilitate raising of funds by the privatized companies for their projects or expansion, in future.

- Disinvestment would bring relief to consumers by way of more choices, and cheaper and better quality of products and services—as has already started happening.
- Opening up the erstwhile public sectors to appropriate private investors would increase economic activity and have an overall beneficial effect on the economy, employment and tax revenues in medium to long-term.

Background Leading to Disinvestment Decision

1. Fiscal deficit of central government

Fiscal Policy is that part of the government policy that is related with raising revenue through taxation and other means and deciding on the level and pattern of expenditure. The fiscal policy operates through the budget.

During 1980s, Indian fiscal situation deteriorated quickly. The reason was an appreciation of current expenditure of the central as well as state governments. A clear view of fiscal situation of Indian central government from 1980-81 onwards is shown in Table 2.1 and Table 2.2. From these two tables, it is clear that the fiscal deficit of both, Centre as well as States is on the increasing trend. Table 2.1 shows the Gross Fiscal Deficit of the Centre and States while Table 2.2 highlights the Select Fiscal Indicators of the central government as Gross Fiscal Deficit (GFD), Gross Primary Deficit (GPD) etc. Analysis of these two tables reveals that fiscal deficit of central government, which was around six per cent during 1980-81, has gone up to eight per cent of GDP during 1990-92. The main reason for India's worst fiscal deficit situation was the increase in Government expenditure, particularly non-plan expenditure (as shown in Table 2.3). During 1990-91, Indian Foreign Exchange (Forex) reserve was little over US $ 1 billion, barely sufficient for one week to finance Indian imports. On the other hand, inflation rate* was on its extreme height of fourteen per cent. These reasons were enough to compel a newly elected government to launch a new set of reforms to stabilize fiscal deficit and to raise resources through disinvestment.

---

* The Inflation Rate is the rate of increase in the price of goods and services over a given period of time. The most generally used measure of inflation is the Consumer Price Index, which is calculated monthly by the Bureau of Labour Statistics.

TABLE 2.1
Gross fiscal deficit (as a percentage of GDP[3])

Year	*Centre*	*States*	*Combined*
1980-81	5.75	2.57	7.5
1981-82	5.11	2.40	6.3
1982-83	5.63	2.64	5.9
1983-84	5.93	2.89	7.3
1984-85	7.05	3.32	9.0
1985-86	7.80	2.68	8.0
1986-87	8.40	2.96	9.9
1987-88	7.61	3.16	9.2
1988-89	7.30	2.76	8.5
1989-90	7.31	3.16	8.9
1990-91	7.85	3.30	9.4

Source: www.fiscalconf.org

TABLE 2.2
Selected fiscal indicators of the Central Government (as per percentage of GDP)*

Year	*Gross fiscal deficit[4] (GFD)*	*Gross primary deficit[5] (GPD)*	*Revenue deficit[6] (RD)*	*Monetized deficit[7] (MD)#*
1980-81	5.75	3.94	2.41	2.46(42.8)
1981-82	5.11	3.23	0.23	2.89(37.0)
1982-83	5.63	3.54	0.69	2.78(32.7)
1983-84	5.93	3.75	2.16	2.80(30.3)
1984-85	7.05	4.63	2.71	2.45(34.8)
1985-86	7.80	5.12	2.10	2.21(28.3)
1986-87	8.40	5.45	2.48	2.26(26.3)
1987-88	7.61	4.44	2.57	2.85(24.3)
1988-89	7.30	3.93	2.48	2.54(20.0)
1989-90	7.31	3.66	2.44	2.83(38.8)
1990-91	7.85	4.07	3.26	2.59(33.0)

Source: Reserve Bank of India, Handbook of statistics, 2000, Table 207.
Notes: *GDP at current market prices with 1993-94 base.
#Figures in parentheses indicate the percentage share of MD to that of GFD.

GRAPH 2.1

Selected fiscal indicators of the Central Government (as a percentage of GDP)

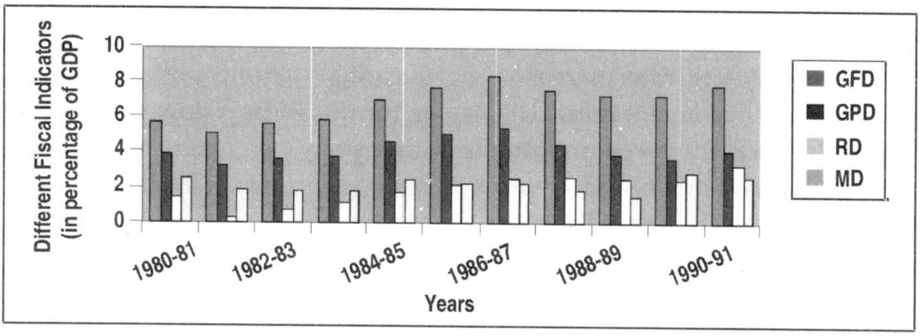

TABLE 2.3

Percentage share of plan and non-plan expenditure in total expenditure

Year	*Plan Expenditure[8] * (PE)*	*Non-plan Expenditure[9] (NPE)*
1984-85	11420.1	5931
1985-86	38	62
1986-87	37	63
1987-88	35	65
1988-89	33	67
1989-90	30	70
1990-91	27	73

Source: National Accounts Statistics, CSO and Economic Survey (1996-97).
Notes: *Includes also Central Assistance for Plans of States and Union Territories.

GRAPH 2.2

Percentage share of plan and non-plan expenditure in total expenditure

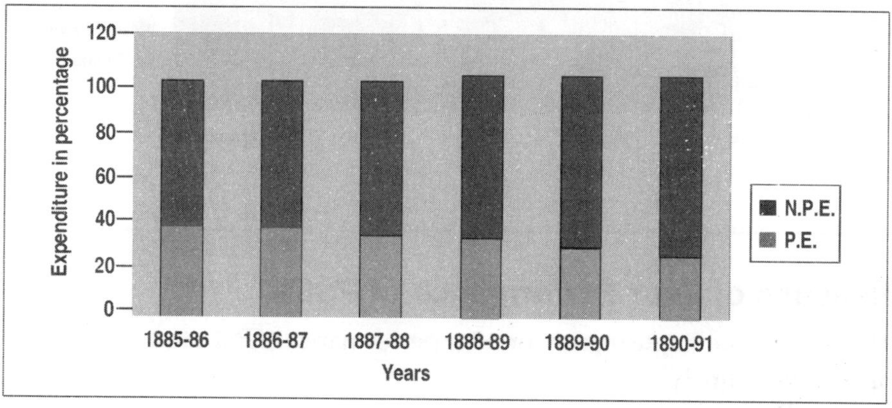

2. Low productivity of investment in PSEs

India's growth rate during 1950-51 to 1980-81 was almost stable but saving and investment rates (at current prices) were more than two times. But in 1980s, the growth rate increased significantly without any increase in savings and investment rates. The reason for this India's slow growth rate was low productivity of investment rather than low rate of saving and investment. Investment and saving as percentage of GDP in the four decades from 1950-51 is shown in Table 2.4

TABLE 2.4
Investment and savings as percentages of GDP

	1950-51	*1960-61*	*1970-71*	*1980-81*	*1989-90*
Investment (Current prices, % of GDP)	10.2	15.7	16.6	22.7	24.1
Investment (Constant 1980-81 prices, % of GDP)	14.7	18.1	18.7	22.7	22.8
Domestic Savings (Current prices, % of GDP)	10.4	12.7	15.7	22.2	22.7
GDP growth (% p.a. 10 years averages)	–	3.6	3.3	3.7	5.7

Source: Joshi & Little (1997).

GRAPH 2.3
Investment and Savings Percentages of GDP

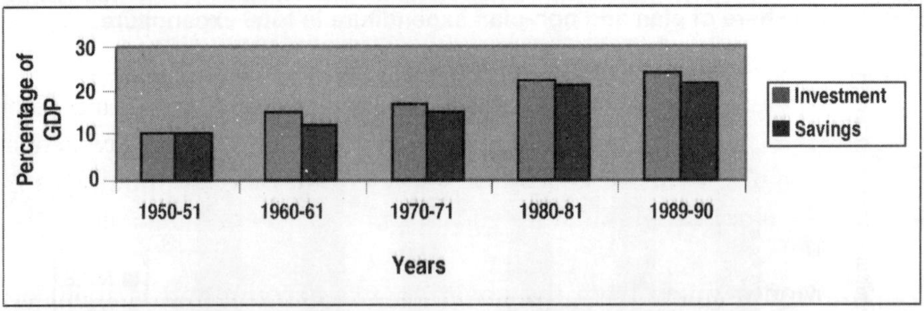

Reasons of Poor Performance of PSEs

There is not one single reason for poor performance of PSEs but a multitude of reasons, namely:

1. Political interference
2. High cost of delay

3. Fear of scams
4. Low rate of ROI
5. Headless plants without CEOs for months
6. Ineffective management
7. Huge inventories
8. Trade unionism
9. Over staffing, bureaucratization leading to excessive delays and wastage of scarce resources.

NOTES

1. In 1997 for the purpose of making some PSEs truly world class entities they were named as 'Navaratnas'. These are: BHEL, BPCL, HPCL, IOC, IPCL, NTPC, ONGC, SAIL & VSNL. Two more PSEs GAIL & MTNL were later given the same status.
2. For making some PSEs efficient and competitive, 97 other profit making PSEs were referred to as Mini-Ratnas.
3. GDP is the total value of goods and services produced by a nation. The total value of all goods and services produced within the boundaries of a particular country in any given year.
4. Fiscal deficit is total expenditure including loans minus (revenue receipts+grants +non-debt capital receipts).
5. Primary deficit is fiscal deficit less interest payments.
6. Revenue deficit is the difference between revenue receipts and revenue expenditures.
7. Monetised deficit is increase in net RBI credit to the central government, comprising to the net increase in the holdings of treasury bills of the RBI and its contribution to the market borrowings of the government.
8. The expenditure of the government can be broken up into Plan and Non-Plan Expenditure. Money given from the government's account for the Central Plan is called Plan Expenditure. This is developmental in nature and is spent on schemes detailed in the Plan.
9. Money given from the government's account and is spent on schemes not mentioned in the Plan.

REFERENCES

1. Drabu, Haseeb A. (1992). *Capital to Output Ratios and Growth: Conceptual Issues and Empirical Evidence* in Arun Ghosh et al. (edited), Indian Industrialisation, Oxford University Press, Delhi.

2. Ganesh, G. (2001). *Privatisation in India,* Mittal, New Delhi.
3. Joshi, Vijay and Little, I. M. D. (1994). *India: Macroeconomics and Political Economy,* 1964-1991, Oxford University Press, Delhi.
4. Kumari, Anita (1993). *Productivity in Public Sector: Analysis at Industry Group Level,* Economic and Political Weekly, Vol. 28, No. 48, November, pp. M145-62.
5. Mani, Sunil. *Disinvestment in Public Sector Enterprises Reforms: Indian Experience since 1991,* Memio Working Paper No. 272, Centre for Development Studies.
6. Mishra, R.K. *Public Enterprises Policy in India,* Kalaiedoscope, August-September, 1999.
7. Mohnot Sr., Edited (1991). *Privatisation—Options and Challenges,* CIER.
8. Nagaraj, R. (1991). *Increase in India's Growth Rate,* Economic and Political Weekly, Vol. 26, No. 15, April 13, (2005): *Disinvestment and Privatisation in India: Assessment and Options,* paper prepared for Asian Development Bank's Policy Networking Project, New Delhi.
9. Narain, Laxmi. *Principles and Practices of Public Enterprises Management,* Sultan Chand, 1994.
10. Prakash, Jagdish (1992). *Privatisation of Public Enterprises in India,* Himalaya Publishing House, Bombay.
11. Saxena, R.N. (1991). *Four Decades of Indian Railways (1950-1990),* Academic Foundation, New Delhi.
12. Singh, Harvinder (2002). *Performance Evaluation of State Enterprise,* Deep and Deep Publications, New Delhi.
13. Thomas, M.K. (2000). *Public Sector Transport in India in the New Millennium: A Historical Perspective,* Ebenezer Publishers, Pune.
14. Website of Ministry of Disinvestment, www.divest.nic.in

CHAPTER 3

Disinvestment Drive in India

Introduction

Privatization, or what is commonly referred to as 'disinvestment', has greatly evolved since the initial policy statements issued by the Government of India (GOI) in the early 1990s. Erstwhile ministries formed at the Centre were quite cynical on hastening the much required process for disinvestment of public sector enterprises (PSEs) because of their lack of political will to counter opposition in Parliament. The populist stance of successive governments continued until Government of India (GOI) formed the Ministry of Disinvestment (MOD) on 10th December, 1999 with a view to establish a systematic policy approach to disinvestment and to give a fresh impetus to the Government's disinvestment program.

Post independence, *i.e.,* after 1950, GOI formed several PSEs with a view to serve a public purpose at a time when there was no substantial private capital in the country to talk of and a virtually non-existent capital market. The MOD's official website admits that: Times have shown that bureaucrats cannot be in business. Despite huge injection of funds in the past decades, poor management, slow decision-making procedures, lack of accountability, etc. have reduced the country's public sector to a symbol of inefficiency, industrial sickness and a drain on the exchequer. Commercial entities need efficient management, quick decisions to withstand the competition of funds and the infusion of funds, none of which it can get as long as it is a PSE. Therefore, it is high time for greater public and private sector participation. This can be achieved by transferring public assets to private players.

Disinvestment: Meaning and Definition

Disinvestment, which has become a universal trend, means transfer of ownership and/or management of an enterprise from the public sector to private hands. It also means the withdrawal of the State from an industry or sector, partially or fully. In another words, disinvestment stands for opening up of an industry that has been reserved for the public sector to the private sector. Therefore, disinvestment simply is the withdrawal of capital from a public corporation. Today, disinvestment is an inevitable historical reaction to the indiscriminate expansion of the public sector and the associated problems. Even in the 'communist' nations it has became a vital measure of economic rejuvenation. In India, although there were some isolated cases of disinvestment in the eighties, no definite policy decision was taken until the new economic policy was ushered in.

Commencement of Disinvestment Process

Through the decade of 1990, there had been increasing consensus on the merits of disinvestment. The New Industrial Policy (announced in July 1991) took bold step regarding the restructuring of public sector through disinvestment, which was an offshoot of Industrial Policy of the Narsimha Rao Government. It is classified into two phases:

- The Initial Phase (December 1991 to August 1999).
- The Second Phase (1999-2000 to 2002-03).

The Initial Phase

Interim budget 1991-92

The policy of the Government on disinvestment has evolved over a period of time and it can be briefly stated in the form of *following statements* made in chronological order.

It has been decided that the Government would disinvest up to twenty per cent of its equity in selected PSEs in favour of mutual funds and financial or investment institutions in the public sector. The disinvestment, which would broad base the equity, improves management and enhances the availability of resources for these enterprises, is also expected to yield Rs. 2,500 crore to the exchequer in 1991-92.

Industrial policy statement of 24th July 1991

It stated that the government would divest part of its holdings in selected PSEs, but did not place any cap on the extent of disinvestment, nor did it restrict disinvestment in favour of any particular class of investors. The objective for disinvestment was stated to provide further market discipline to the performance of public enterprises.

Budget speech (1991-92)

"In this pronouncement, the cap of 20% for disinvestment was reinstated and the eligible investors' universe was again modified to consist of mutual funds and investment institutions in the public sector and the workers in these firms. The objectives too were modified, the modified objectives being: 'to raise resources, encourage wider public participation and promote greater accountability'.

In order to raise resources, Government equity in selected PSEs would be offered to mutual funds and investment institutions in the public sector, and also to workers in these firms".

Disinvestment in 1991-92

In the budget speech for 1991-92, the government decided to divest up to 20% of its equity in selected PSEs to yield Rs. 2,500 crore. For selection of PSEs, a steering committee was constituted. Department of Public Enterprises (DPEs) under the Ministry of Industry coordinated all activities in this regard.

Under two tranches of disinvestment, first in December 1991 and second in February 1992, Rs. 3,038 crore was realized during 1991-92. The details of PSEs disinvested in 1991-92 with number of disinvested shares are given in Table 3.1.

TABLE 3.1
PSEs disinvested in 1991-92

Year	*No. of companies in which equity sold*	*Target receipt for the year (Rs. in crore)*	*Actual receipt (Rs. in crore)*	*Methodology*
1991-92	47 (31 in first tranche and 16 in second tranche)	2500	3038	Minority shares sold by auction method in bundles of 'very good', 'good' and 'average' companies.

Source: Department of Disinvestment. *Website*: www.divest.nic.in

Disinvestment in 1992-93

According to the announcement made in the budget speech for 1992-93, Rs. 3,500 crore was to be raised by disinvestment of shares in public sector companies during the financial year. A total amount of Rs. 1,913 crore was realized in three tranches during 1992-93 against a target of Rs. 3,500 crore. The details are given in Table 3.2.

TABLE 3.2
Amount realised from disinvestment in 1992-93

Month	*No. of PSEs disinvested*	*No. of shares sold (in crore)*	*Amount realised (Rs. in crore)*
Oct. 1992	8	12.87	683.95
Dec. 1992	12	33.06	1183.83
March 1993	9	3.01	46.63
Total	29	44.94	1912.51

Source: Department of Disinvestment. *Website:* www.divest.nic.in

Report of the Rangarajan committee on disinvestment of shares in PSEs: April 1993

The Rangarajan Committee recommendations emphasized the need for substantial disinvestment. It stated that the percentage of equity to be divested could be up to 49% for industries explicitly reserved for the public sector. It recommended that in exceptional cases such as the enterprises, which had a dominant market share or where separate identity had to be maintained for strategic reasons, the target public ownership level could be kept at 26%, *i.e.*, disinvestment could take place to the extent of 74%. In all other cases, it recommended 100% disinvestment of the government stake. Holding of 51% or more equity by the government was recommended only for following six schedule industries, namely:

I. Coal and Lignite
II. Minerals oils
III. Arms, ammunition and defence equipment
IV. Atomic energy
V. Radioactive minerals
VI. Railway transport

However, the Government did not take any decision on the recommendations of the Rangarajan Committee.

Disinvestment in 1993-94

Although the target was set for Rs. 3,500 crore, the government could not go in for further sale of shares of PSEs due to unfavourable stock market conditions throughout 1993-94.

Disinvestment in 1994-95

Due to adverse stock market conditions and other related factors, no disinvestment of PSEs shares could take place during 1993-94, an advertisement for sale of shares in some PSEs was realized in the month of March 1994. The target for this financial year was fixed for realization of Rs. 4,000 crore from disinvestment. Against fixed target of Rs. 4,000 crore, an amount of Rs. 4,843.07 crore was realized in three tranches:

First Tranche (March/April 1994)

After considering the stock market conditions, the government decided to off-load shares in respect of seven PSEs in March 1994. As per the fixed criterion, bids were accepted for sale amounting to around Rs. 2,282 crore in six companies. The details of the PSEs disinvested are given below in Table 3.3.

TABLE 3.3
PSEs disinvested in March/April 1994

Sl. No.	*Name of the enterprise*	*No. of shares sold (in crore)*	*% of total no. of shares of the PSEs*	*Amount of sale (Rs. in crore)*
1.	Bharat Electronics Ltd.	0.331	4.14	47.17
2.	BEML	0.150	4.07	48.27
3.	Bharat Heavy Electronics Ltd.	2.692	13.74	303.34
4.	Hindustan Petroleum Corporation Ltd.	0.447	7.00	563.11
5.	Mahanagar Telephone Nigam Ltd.	7.694	12.82	1322.17
6.	National Aluminium Co Ltd.	0.003	0.04	0.096
	Total	13.317		2282.156

Source: Enterprise Survey, 1995-96, Vol. I, p. 197.

Second Tranche (October 1994)

In October 1994, a notice inviting tenders was issued for sale of shares in seven PSEs. However, sales were affected in six PSEs as no shares could be sold of MTNL. The details of sales affected are given in Table 3.4.

TABLE 3.4
PSEs disinvested in October 1994

Sl. No.	Name of the enterprise	No. of shares sold (in crore)	% of total no. of shares of the PSEs	Amount of sale (Rs. in crore)
1.	Container Corporation of India	3.299	20.00	99.71
2.	Indian Oil Corporation	3.443	3.77	1028.11
3.	National Fertilizer Ltd.	0.007	0.01	0.28
4.	Oil and Natural Gas Commission	0.682	2.00	1053.52
5.	Steel Authority of India Ltd.	0.372	0.41	22.66
6.	Shipping Corporation of India Ltd.	0.387	3.37	28.08
	Total	4.194		2230.36

Source: Public Enterprise Survey, 1995-996, Vol. I, p. 195.

Third Tranche of disinvestment (January 1995)

During January 1995, an amount of Rs. 330 crore was realized from disinvestment of five PSEs. Though shares of six PSEs were offered for sale but only five were disinvested as the government decided not to sell shares of Videsh Sanchar Nigam Limited (VSNL). The details of the PSEs disinvested are given in Table 3.5.

TABLE 3.5
PSEs disinvested in January 1995

Sl. No.	Name of the enterprise	% of total no. of shares of the PSEs	Amount of sale (Rs. in crore)
1.	Engineers India Ltd.	5.99	67.53
2.	Gas Authority of India Ltd.	3.37	194.12
3.	ITDC	10.00	53.99
4.	Indian Oil Corporation Ltd.	0.03	5.54
5.	Kudremukh Iron Ore Co. Ltd.	0.97	13.39
	Total		330.57

Source: Public Enterprise Survey, 1995-96, Vol. I.

The common minimum programme of the united front government: 1996

The highlights of the policy formulated by the United Front Government were as follows:

- To carefully examine the public sector non-core strategic areas;
- To set up a Disinvestment Commission for advising on the disinvestment related matters;
- To take and implement decisions to disinvest in a transparent manner;
- Job security, opportunities for re-training and re-deployment to be assured;
- No disinvestment objective was, however, mentioned in the policy statement.

Disinvestment commission recommendations: Feb. 1997–Oct. 1999

Pursuant to the above policy of the United Front Government, a Disinvestment Commission was set up in 1996. By August 1999, it made recommendations on fifty eight PSEs. The recommendations indicated a shift from public offerings to strategic/trade sales, with transfer of management.

Disinvestment in 1996-97

The budget for 1996-97 had taken a credit for an amount of Rs. 5,000 crore for mobilization of resources through disinvestment of PSEs' shares. The government considered names of companies from the communication and petroleum sector for the purpose of disinvestment of PSEs' shares and finally decided to take up two PSEs (VSNL and IOC). While both VSNL and Indian Oil Corporation (IOC) were allocated, and preparatory work had also been initiated for the GDR issue[1], but due to some unfavourable market conditions, only VSNL could be taken up for disinvestment (in GDR) during this period. The details are shown in Table 3.6.

TABLE 3.6
PSEs disinvested in 1996-97

Year	*No. of companies in which equity sold*	*Target receipt for the year (Rs. in crore)*	*Actual receipts (Rs. in crore)*	*Methodology*
1996-97	1(VSNL)	5000	380	GDR (VSNL) in international market

Source: Department of Disinvestment. *Website:* www.divest.nic.in

Disinvestment in 1997-98

In the budget speech for 1997-98, a target of Rs. 4,800 crore was fixed for mobilization of resources through disinvestment of PSEs shares. This target was to be achieved by disinvestment in MTNL, GAIL, CONCOR and IOC. Due to unfavourable conditions in the international market, it was decided to defer the issues of GAIL, CONCOR & IOC and a GDR issue of MTNL was offered in the international market in the month of November 1997 and amount of Rs. 902 crore was realized. The details are given in Table 3.7.

TABLE 3.7
PSEs disinvested in 1997-98

Year	*No. of companies in which equity sold*	*Target receipt for the year (Rs. in crore)*	*Actual receipts (Rs. in crore)*	*Methodology*
1997-98	1 (MTNL)	4800	902	GDR (MTNL) in international market

Source: Department of Disinvestment. *Website:* www.divest.nic.in

The Second Phase

Budget speech (1998-99)

In its first budgetary pronouncement, the new government decided to bring down government shareholding in the PSEs to 26% in the generality of cases (thus facilitating ownership changes, as was recommended by the Disinvestment Commission). It, however, stated that the government would retain majority holdings in PSEs involving strategic considerations and that the interests of the workers would be protected in all cases.

Disinvestment in 1998-99

The budget speech for 1998-99 had taken a credit for an amount of Rs. 5,000 crore to be realized through disinvestment of PSEs' shares. This target was to be achieved by disinvestment in GAIL, VSNL, CONCOR, IOC and ONGC. An amount of Rs. 5,371 crore was realized during the said period. The details of these disinvested shares is given in Table 3.8.

TABLE 3.8
PSEs disinvested in 1998-99

Sl. No.	*Name of enterprise*	*No. of shares disinvested (in crore)*	*Amount realised (Rs. in crore)*
1.	CONCOR	0.9000	223.65
2.	GAIL	13.1690	673.86
3.	IOC	3.1272	1208.96
4.	VSNL	3.0000	783.68
5.	ONGC	15.3068	2484.96
	Total	33.5630	5373.11

Source: Department of Disinvestment. *Website:* www.divest.nic.in

Budget speech (1999-2000)

Government's strategy towards public sector enterprises will continue to encompass a judicious mix of strengthening strategic units, privatizing non-strategic ones through gradual disinvestment or strategic sale and devising viable rehabilitation strategies for weak units. One highlight of the policy was that the expression **'privatization'** was used for the first time.

Strategic and Non-strategic classification

On 16th March 1999, the government classified the PSEs into strategic and non-strategic areas for the purpose of disinvestment. It was decided that the strategic PSEs would be those in the areas of:

- Arms and ammunition and the allied items of defence equipment, defence aircrafts and warships;
- Atomic energy (except in the areas related to the generation of nuclear power and applications of radiation and radioisotopes to agriculture, medicine and non-strategic industries); and
- Railway transport.

All other public sector enterprises were to be considered non-strategic. For the non-strategic PSEs, it was decided that the reduction of the government stake to 26% would not be automatic and the manner and the pace of doing so would be worked out on a case-to-case basis. A decision in regard to the percentage of disinvestment, *i.e.,* the government stake going down to less than 51% or to 26%, would be taken on the following considerations:

- Whether the industrial sector requires the presence of the public sector as a countervailing force to prevent concentration of power in private hands and

- Whether the industrial sector requires a proper regulatory mechanism to protect the consumer interests before PSEs are privatized.

Disinvestment in 1999-2000

The budget speech for 1999-2000 had taken a target for an amount of Rs. 10,000 crore to be realized through disinvestment of PSEs' shares. The total amount of Rs. 1,818 crore was realized through GDR issue of GAIL, domestic issues of VSNL and other strategic sales. The details are given in Table 3.9.

TABLE 3.9
PSEs disinvested in 1999-2000

Sl. No.	*Name of enterprise*	*No. of shares disinvested (in crore)*	*Amount realised (Rs. in crore)*
1.	GAIL	13.5000	945.00
2.	IOC	0.4212	162.79
3.	ONGC	3.8266	296.48
4.	VSNL	0.1000	75.00
5.	MFIL (Modern Food Industries Ltd.)	0.0920	94.51
	Total	15.9398	1573.78

Source: Department of Disinvestment. *Website:* www.divest.nic.in.

Budget speech (2000-2001)

The highlights of the policy for the year 2000-01 were that for the first time the government made the statement that it was prepared to reduce its stake in the non-strategic PSEs even below 26% if necessary, that there would be increasing emphasis on strategic sales and that the entire proceeds from disinvestment/privatization would be deployed in social sectors, restructuring of PSEs and retirement of public debt. The main elements of the policy are reiterated as follows:

- To restructure and revive potentially viable PSEs;
- To close down PSEs which cannot be revived;
- To bring down the government equity in all non-strategic PSEs to 26% or lower, if necessary;
- To fully protect the interests of workers;
- To emphasize increasingly on strategic sales of identified PSEs; and
- To use the entire receipt from disinvestment and privatization for meeting expenditure in social sectors, restructuring of PSEs and retiring public debt.

In line with this policy during the last two years, the government has approved financial restructuring of twenty PSEs, and has recently established a new department for disinvestment to launch a systematic policy approach to disinvestment and privatization and to give a fresh impetus to this programme. As a result, many public sector enterprises have been able to restructure their operations, improve productivity and achieve a turnaround in performance. Government has recently approved a comprehensive package for restructuring of SAIL, one of our Navaratna PSEs.

There are many PSEs, which are sick and are not capable of being revived. The only remaining option is to close down these undertakings after providing an acceptable safety net for the employees and workers.

Excerpts from the address by the president to the joint session of parliament (February, 2001)

"The public sector has played a vital role in the development of our economy. However, the nature of this role cannot remain frozen to what it was conceived fifty years ago — a time when the technological landscape and the national and international economic environment were so very different. The private sector in India has come of age, contributing substantially to our nation-building process. Therefore, both the public sector and the private sector need to be viewed as mutually complementary parts of the national sector. The private sector must assume greater public responsibilities just as the public sector needs to focus more on achieving results in a highly competitive market. While some public enterprises are making profits, quite a few have accumulated huge losses. With public finances under intense pressure, governments are just not able to sustain them much longer. Accordingly, the centre as well as several state governments is compelled to embark on a programme of disinvestment.

The Government's approach to PSEs has a three-fold objective:

- Revival of potentially viable enterprises;
- Closing down of those PSEs that cannot be revived; and
- Bringing down the government equity in non-strategic PSEs to 26% or lower.

The government has decided to disinvest a substantial part of its equity in enterprises such as Air India, ITDC, IPCL, VSNL, CMC, BALCO, and MUL. Wherever necessary, strategic partners would be selected through a transparent process."

Disinvestment in 2000-01

In the budget speech for the year 2000-01, against the target of Rs. 10,000 crore, only Rs. 1,868.73 crore were recovered from the public offer of four PSEs *viz.*, BALCO, LJMC, CPCL and BRPL. The details of disinvested enterprises are shown in Table 3.10.

TABLE 3.10
PSEs disinvested in 2000-01

Sl. No.	*Name of companies in which equity sold*	*Actual receipts (Rs. in crore)*	*Methodology*
1.	BALCO	553.50	Strategic sale of 51% shares
2.	BRPL and Chennai Refineries	658.13	Takeover by IOC
3.	Kochi Refinery	659.10	Takeover by BPCL
	Total	1868.73	

Source: Department of Disinvestment. *Website:* www.divest.nic.in.

Budget Speech (2001-2002)

To use the proceeds for providing:

- Restructuring assistance to PSEs
- Safety net to workers
- Reduction of debt burden

"Given the advanced stage of the process of disinvestment in many of these companies, I am emboldened to take credit for a receipt of Rs. 12,000 crore from disinvestment during the next year. An amount of Rs. 7,000 crore out of this will be used for providing restructuring assistance to PSEs, safety net to workers and reduction of debt burden. A sum of Rs. 5,000 crore will be used to provide additional budgetary support for the plan primarily in the social and infrastructure sectors. This additional allocation for the plan will be contingent upon realisation of the anticipated receipts."

Excerpts from the address by the president to the joint session of parliament (February, 2002)

"The public sector has played a laudable role in enabling our country to achieve the national objective of self reliance. However, the significantly changed economic environment that now prevails both in India and globally makes it imperative for both the public and the private sector to become competitive. Learning from our experience, especially over the last decade, it is evident that disinvestment in public sector enterprises is no longer a matter of choice, but is imperative. The prolonged fiscal haemorrhage from the majority of these enterprises cannot be sustained any longer. The disinvestment policy and the transparent procedures adopted for disinvestment have now been widely accepted and the shift in emphasis from disinvestment of minority shares to strategic sale has yielded excellent results. The Government has taken two major initiatives to improve the safety net for the workers of PSEs:

(i) Enhanced Voluntary Retirement Scheme (VRS) benefits in those PSEs where wage revision had not taken place in 1992 or 1997.

(ii) Increased training opportunities for self-employment for workers retiring under VRS."

Disinvestment in 2001-02

The budget speech for 2001-02 had taken a credit of Rs. 12,000 crore from disinvestment of VSNL, IBP, PPL, ITDC, HCI, STC and MMTC. Against the target of Rs. 12,000 crore, only Rs. 5,632 crore was recovered. The details of these transactions are given in Table 3.11.

TABLE 3.11
PSEs disinvested in 2001-02

Year	*No. of companies in which equity sold*	*Target receipt for the year (Rs. in crore)*	*Actual receipts (Rs. in crore)*	*Methodology*
2001-02	9	12,000	5,632	Strategic sale of CMC—51%, HTL—74%, VSNL—25%, IBP—33.58%, PPL—74%, and sale by other modes: ITDC &

Source: Department of Disinvestment. *Website:* www.divest.nic.in.

Excerpts from the budget speech for 2002-03 of the Finance Minister

Privatization

"With the streamlined procedure for disinvestment and privatization, I am happy to report that the Government has now completed strategic sales in seven public sector companies and some hotels' properties of HCI and ITDC. The change in approach from the disinvestment of small lots of shares to strategic sales of blocks of shares to strategic investors has improved the price earning ratios obtained. We expect to complete the disinvestment in another six companies and the remaining hotels in HCI and ITDC this year. Disinvestment receipts for the present year are estimated at Rs 5,000 crore excluding the special dividend from VSNL of Rs. 1,887 crore. Encouraged by these results, I am once again taking credit for a receipt of Rs. 12,000 crore from disinvestment next year."

Disinvestment in 2002-03

In the budget speech for 2002-03, a target of Rs. 12,000 crore was fixed for mobilization of resources through disinvestment of seven PSEs shares. However, only Rs. 3,348 crore were realized during the said period. The details of the disinvested shares are shown in Table 3.12 and Table 3.13.

TABLE 3.12
PSEs disinvested in 2002-03

Year	*No. of companies in which equity sold*	*Target receipt for the year (Rs. in crore)*	*Actual receipts (Rs. in crore)*	*Methodology*
2002-03	7	12,000	3,348	Strategic sale: HZL — 26%, MFIL—26%, IPCL — 25%, HCI, ITDC, and Maruti: control premium from renunciation of rights issue, ESOP: HZL, CMC.

Source: Department of Disinvestment. *Website:* www.divest.nic.in

TABLE 3.13
Details of disinvestment proceeds during 2002-03

Sl. No.	*Name of PSEs*	*Percentage of equity disinvested (%)*	*Proceeds realised (Rs. in crore)*
1.	Hindustan Zinc Ltd.	26 + 3.46*	451
2.	Maruti Udyog Ltd.	4.2**	1000
3.	IPCL	26	1491
4.	MFIL	26	44
5.	ITDC	100	273
6.	Hotel Corporation of India (Ten Hotels)	100	83
7.	Computer Maintenance Corporation (CMC)	6.06*	6.07
	Total		3348.07

*This per cent equity was disinvested in favour of employees.
**4.2% reduction from 49.74 through rights offer renunciation and control premium.

Excerpts from the budget speech for 2003-04 of the finance minister

"I am confident that the pace of disinvestment will accelerate in the coming year. I wish to also state that details about the already announced Disinvestment Fund and Asset Management Company (AMC) to hold residual shares post-disinvestment, shall be finalized early in 2003-04......., disinvestment is not merely for mobilizing revenues for the Government, it is mainly for unlocking the productive potential of these undertakings, and for reorienting the Government away from business and towards the business of governance."

Disinvestment in 2003-04

In the budget speech for 2003-04, the Finance Minister Jaswant Singh announced a target of Rs. 13,200 crore from disinvestment of the government held equity in public sector companies. This was proposed to be achieved by disinvestment in nine public sector companies like IPCL, CMC, GAIL, and ONGC etc. This was the first time when actual receipt was comparatively more than predetermined target. An amount of Rs. 15,547 crore was recovered against the target of Rs. 13,200 crore as per details given in Table 3.14.

TABLE 3.14
PSEs disinvested in 2003-04

Year	*No. of companies in which equity sold*	*Target receipt for the year (Rs . in crore)*	*Actual receipts (Rs. in crore)*	*Methodology*
2003-04	9	13,200	15,547	Maruti—IPO (27.5%), Jessop & Co. Ltd. (Strategic sale—72%), HZL (Call Option of SP — 18.92%), Public Offers—IPCL (28.95%), CMC (26%), IBP (26%), DRDG (20%), GAIL (10%), ONGC (10%), ICI (9.2%)

Source: Department of Disinvestment. *Website:* www.divest.nic.in

Disinvestment in 2004-05

In the budget speech for 2004-05, a target of Rs. 4,000 crore is fixed for mobilization of resources through disinvestment of PSEs' shares. However, so far only 2,684 crore has been realized through an Initial Public Offer (IPO) of NTPC. The details of the disinvested shares are shown in Table 3.15.

TABLE 3.15
PSEs disinvested in 2004-05

Year	No. of companies in which equity sold	Target receipt for the year (Rs. in crore)	Actual receipts (Rs. in crore)	Methodology
2004-05	3	4,000	2,765	NTPC (IPO) (5.25%), IPCL (5%) to employees, ONGC (0.01%)

Source: Department of Disinvestment. *Website:* www.divest.nic.in

Disinvestment in 2004-05

As due to left parties pressure, in the year 2005-06 as such no fixed target was fixed for mobilization of resources through disinvestment of PSEs' shares. But still by sale of shares to Public Sector Financial Institutions & Public Sector Banks on *'Differential Pricing Method'*, Rs. 1567.60 were recovered as shown in Table 3.16 while Table 3.17 shows the strategic sale of PSEs year 2000 onwards.

TABLE 3.16
PSEs disinvested in 2005-06

Year	No. of companies in which equity sold	Target receipt for the year (Rs. in crore)	Actual receipts (Rs. in crore)	Methodology
2004-05			1567.60	By sale of shares to Public Sector Financial Institutions & Public Sector Banks on 'Differential Pricing Method'

Source: Department of Disinvestment. *Website:* www.divest.nic.in

TABLE 3.17
Strategic sale of PSEs year 2000 onwards

Sl. No.	Name of the PSE	Date	Ratio of paid up equity sold %	Face value of equity sold (Rs. in crore)	Realization (Rs. in crore)
1a.	MFIL	Jan. 2000	74	9.63	105.45
1b.	MFIL – Phase-II		26	3.38	44.07
2.	LJMC	July-2000	74	0.70	2.53
3.	BALCO ^	Mar. 2001	51	112.52	826.50
4a.	CMC	Oct. 2001	51	7.73	152.00

(Contd.)

4b.	CMC $		61	0.91	6.07
5.	HTL	Oct. 2001	74	13.10	55.00
6.	VSNL ^	Feb. 2002	25	73.20	3689.00
7.	IBP	Feb. 2002	33.6	7.40	1153.68
8.	PPL	Feb. 2002	74	320.10	153.70
9.	Jessop	Aug. 2003	74	68.10	18.18
10a.	HZL	Apr. 2002	26	109.80	445.00
10b.	HZL*	Nov. 2003	18.92	79.90	323.88
10c.	HZL $	Apr. 2003	3.5	6.17	6.19
11.	IPCL	May 2002	26	64.50	1490.84
12a.	MUL Phase I	Mar. 2002	–	–	1000.00
12b.	MUL Phase II	July 2003	27.5	39.73	993.34
13.	(STC)#	Mar. 2003			40.00
14.	MMTC Ltd.#	Mar. 2003			60.00
15-17.	HCI (3 Hotels)	2001-02 various dates	100	14.70	242.51
18-36.	ITDC (19 Hotels)	2001-02 various dates	100	27.10	444.17
37.	ICI	Oct. 2003	9.2	3.76	77.10
38.	IPCL	Mar. 2004	28.95	73.85	1202.85
39.	IBP Co. Ltd.	Mar. 2004	26	5.80	350.66
40.	CMC Ltd.	Mar. 2004	26.25	3.98	190.44
41.	DCI	Mar. 2004	20	5.60	223.20
42.	GAIL	Mar. 2004	10	84.60	1627.36
43.	ONGC	Mar. 2004	10	142.60	10542.40

Source: Annual Report (2002-2003), Ministry of Disinvestment & Department of Disinvestment. *Website:* www.divest.nic.in

Notes: ^Including dividend & dividend tax/withdrawal of surplus cash prior to disinvestment.

* Realization from call option.

$ Disinvestment in favour of employees.

#The receipt is on account of transfer of cash reserves.

Position till 2005-2006

Enterprisewise details showing target receipt, amount realized number of shares disinvested etc. is given in Appendix 'B'. The appendix indicates the actual disinvestment from 1991-92 till date, the methodologies adopted for such disinvestment and the extent of disinvestment in different CPSEs. It reveals since the beginning of disinvestment in 1991-92, a total amount of Rs. 49,214.03 crore have been realized till FY 2005-06.

Disinvestment in states

There are good reasons for thinking disinvestment, since change from public to private will have significant effects on its performance. More particularly, disinvestment reduces political influence and increases the influence of capital market factors. Therefore, a number of states in India have also started disinvestment of their state level public enterprises (SLPEs). Some of the states like Punjab have also set up their state level disinvestment commissions as a part of their economic policy. Table 3.18 exemplifies the disinvestment attempts in the states, Table 3.19 illustrates status of investment in SLPEs, as on 31st March 2003, while Table 3.20 shows the details of enterprises, which are under study by the disinvestment commission.

TABLE 3.18
Disinvestment in states

Sl. No.	*Name of the state*	*Approximate no. of SLPEs**	*SLPEs identified for disinvestment winding up/ restructuring*	*No. of SLPEs in which process initiated*	*No. of SLPEs privatized*	*No. of SLPEs closed down*
1.	Andhra Pradesh	128	87	79	13	38
2.	Arunachal Pradesh	7	N/A	N/A	N/A	N/A
3.	Assam	42	N/A	N/A	N/A	N/A
4.	Bihar	54	6	6	N/A	N/A
5.	Delhi	15	N/A	1	1	N/A
6.	Gujarat	50	24	24	3	6
7.	Haryana	45	8	6	1	4
8.	Himachal Pradesh	21	15	8	3	2
9.	Jammu & Kashmir	20	7	2	N/A	N/A
10.	Karnataka	85	39	20	2	12
11.	Kerala	111	55	40	N/A	10
12.	Madhya Pradesh	26	14	14	1	N/A
13.	Maharashtra	66	11	4	N/A	N/A
14.	Manipur	14	10	N/A	N/A	N/A
15.	Mizoram	5	N/A	N/A	N/A	N/A
16.	Orissa	72	33	10	9	11

*State Level Public Enterprises.

(Contd.)

17.	Punjab	53	11	11	1	6
18.	Rajasthan	28	10	6	1	1
19.	Sikkim	12	N/A	N/A	N/A	N/A
20.	Tamil Nadu	59	29	29	N/A	7
21.	Uttar Pradesh	41	25	25	1	14
22.	West Bengal	82	15	15	N/A	N/A
	Total	1036	399	300	36	111

N/A —Not available.
Source: State Governments/IPE, Hyderabad.

TABLE 3.19
Status of investment in SLPEs (as on 33.03.2003)

Sl. No.	*Name of the state*	*Approximate no. of SLPEs*	*Estimated total investment in SLPEs (Rs. in crore)*	*Net Accumulated loss* (Rs. in crore)*	*Approximate number of loss making SLPEs*	*Approximate number of non-working SLPEs*
1.	Andhra Pradesh	128	48794	2919	62	9
2.	Arunachal Pradesh	7	14	14	3	2
3.	Assam	42	3732	2885	36	10
4.	Bihar	54	8169	5060	12	28
5.	Delhi	15	10964	6995	3	N/A
6.	Gujarat	50	25758	6774	24	10
7.	Haryana	45	443	384	10	4
8.	Himachal Pradesh	21	4731	605	13	2
9.	Jammu & Kashmir	20	1948	587	16	1
10.	Karnataka	85	27813	1888	30	7
11.	Kerala	111	16429	3510	52	13
12.	Madhya Pradesh	26	7923	600	8	15
13.	Maharashtra	66	20855	1775	44	18
14.	Manipur	14	81	N/A	10	N/A
15.	Mizoram	5	62	15	4	N/A
16.	Orissa	72	7297	2372	22	24
17.	Punjab	53	13384	1435	25	28
18.	Rajasthan	28	11576	315	11	8
19.	Sikkim	12	121	29	6	3
20.	Tamil Nadu	59	6192	N/A	33	N/A
21.	Uttar Pradesh	41	17773	5327	21	19
22.	West Bengal	82	18183	7062	62	8
	Total	1036	252242	50551	507	209

N/A — Not available.
Source: State Government, CAG Reports.
Notes: *The figures indicated are only of those SLPEs, which have finalized their accounts (could be only 25–30% of the total companies).

TABLE 3.20
Enterprises under study by disinvestment commission

Sl. No.	Name of public sector enterprises
1.	Balmer and Lawrie Co. Ltd.
2.	Bharat Heavy Plates and Vessels (BHPV) Ltd.
3.	Bharat Opthalmic Glass Ltd. (BOGL)
4.	Bharat Petroleum Company Ltd. (BPCL)
5.	Braithwaite and Co. Ltd.
6.	Burn Standard Company Ltd. (BSCL)
7.	Central Inland Water Transport Corporation (CIWTC) Ltd.
8.	Engineering Projects (India) Ltd. (EPIL)
9.	Engineers India Ltd. (EIL)
10.	Fertilizers and Chemicals (Travancore) Ltd. (FACT)
11.	Hindustan Copper Ltd. (HCL)
12.	Hindustan Organic Chemicals Ltd. (HOCL)
13.	Hindustan Paper Corporation (HPC) Ltd.
14.	Hindustan Petroleum Co. Ltd. (HPCL)
15.	Hindustan Salts Ltd. (HSL)
16.	Hotel Corporation of India Ltd. (HCIL)
17.	Indian Medicines Pharmaceuticals Corporation Ltd. (MPCL)
18.	Indian Tourism Development Corporation (ITDC)
19.	Instrumentation Ltd. (IL)
20.	Madras Fertilizers Ltd. (MFL)
21.	Manganese Ore India Ltd.
22.	Maruti Udyog Ltd. (MUL)
23.	MECON Ltd.
24.	Minerals and Metals Trading Corporation (MMTC) of India Ltd.
25.	MSTC Ltd.
26.	National Aluminium Company (NALCO) Ltd.
27.	National Building Construction Corporation (NBCC) Ltd.
28.	National Fertilizers Ltd. (NFL)
29.	National Instruments Ltd. (NIL)
30.	NEPA Ltd.
31.	Rashtriya Chemicals and Fertilizers Ltd. (RCFL)
32.	Shipping Corporation of India (SCI) Ltd.
33.	Sponge Iron India Ltd. (SIIL)
34.	State Trading Corporation (STC)
35.	Tungabhadra Steel Product Ltd.
36.	Tyre Corporation of India Ltd.

Overview of procedure

The procedure followed by the Government of India for disinvestment seeks administrative simplicity and speed of decision making without compromising on transparency and fair play. The process is as follows:

- Proposals for disinvestment in any public sector enterprise based on the recommendations of the Disinvestment Commission or in accordance with the declared Disinvestment Policy of the government are placed for consideration to the Cabinet Committee on Disinvestment (CCD).
- After CCD clears the disinvestment proposal, selection of the Advisor is done through a competitive bidding process.
- After receipt of the Expression of Interest (EOI) in pursuance of Advertisement in newspapers/websites, advisors are selected based on the objective screening in the light of announced criteria/requirements.
- Bidders are invited through advertisement in newspapers to submit their EOI. On receiving the EOI from bidders, the advisors after due diligence of the PSE, prepare the information memorandum in consultation with the concerned PSE. This is given to the short listed prospective bidders who have entered into a confidentiality agreement. The list of bidders is prepared after scrutiny of EOIs and those are shortlisted who meet the prescribed qualification criteria.
- The draft share purchase agreement and the shareholder agreement are also prepared by the Advisor with the help of the legal Advisors, and the final draft is prepared after detailed consultation with the bidders in consultation with the Inter-Ministerial Group (IMG).
- The prospective bidders undertake due diligence of the PSE and hold discussions with the Advisor/the government/the representatives of the PSE for any clarifications.
- Concurrently, the task of valuation of the PSE is undertaken in accordance with the standard national and international practices.
- Based on the feedback received from the prospective bidders, the Share Purchase Agreement (SPA) and Shareholders' Agreement (SHA) are finalised by IMG. After getting them vetted by the Ministry of Law, they are approved by the government (CCD). Thereafter, they are sent to the prospective bidders for inviting their final binding financial bids.
- The material for finalizing upset price is taken from the advisors after receipt of financial bids. The bids are not opened at this stage and are sealed after receipt in presence of bidders. Inter-ministerial

'Evaluation Committee' and the IMG thereafter complete 'upset price' determination exercise. The sealed bids are then opened by IMG in presence of bidders and compared with the 'upset price.'

- After examination, analysis and evaluation, the recommendations of the IMG are placed before the Core Group of Secretaries on Disinvestment (CGD), whose recommendations are placed before the CCD for a final decision regarding selection of the strategic partner, signing of the Share Purchase Agreement and Shareholders' Agreement, and other related issues. In case the disinvested PSEs' shares are listed on the Stock Exchange, an open offer would be required to be made by the bidder before closing the transaction, as per Securities and Exchange Board of India (SEBI) guidelines: Takeover code.
- In the disinvestment process mentioned above, Ministry of Disinvestment is assisted at each stage by an IMG, headed by Secretary (Disinvestment) and comprising officers from the Ministry of Finance, Department of Public Enterprises, the Administrative Ministry/Department controlling the PSE, Department of Company Affairs, Department of Legal Affairs, Chairman and Managing Director (CMD)/Director (Finance) of the company being disinvested, and the Advisors and the Legal Advisors.
- After the transaction is completed, all papers and documents relating to it are turned over to the Comptroller and Auditor General (CAG) of India; the CAG prepares an evaluation for sending it to Parliament and releasing to the public. *The process flow chart on the next page shows the various stages of a typical privatization transaction through strategic sale route.*

Contribution of Disinvestment Proceeds in Meeting Fiscal Deficit

Privatization benefits the society in several ways, one of the main advantages of disinvestment is that it reduces the fiscal burden of the government by relieving it of the losses of the SOEs. To study whether disinvestment fulfils the objective or not, a table regarding the proceeds of disinvestment and its relation to fiscal deficit and internal debt is shown in Tables 3.21 & 3.22. Total disinvestment proceeds since 1991-92 are Rs. 47,831 crore and the total fiscal deficit is about Rs. 11,01,645 crore. It means on an average only 4.33 per cent of the Fiscal Deficit has been financed through disinvestment and contribution of disinvestment proceeds is negligible in retiring international debt on account of market borrowings.

Disinvestment Process Flow Chart

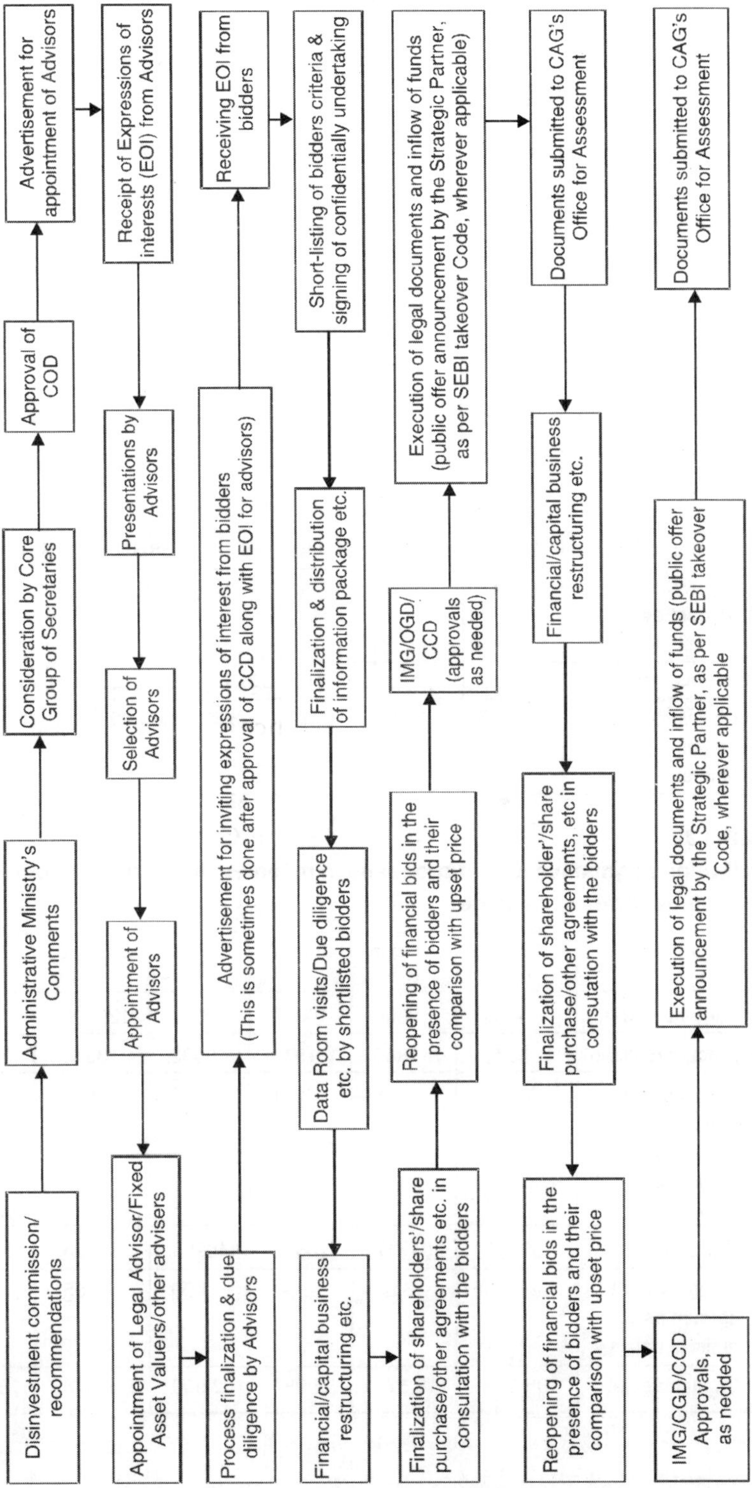

Source: Idea taken from Disinvestment Commission's annual report (2002-20030, Ministry of Disinvestment (pp. 14-15).

TABLE 3.21

Contributions of disinvestment proceeds in meeting fiscal deficit from FY 1991-92 to 1997-98 (Amount in crore)

Sl. No.	*Details*	*1991-92*	*1992-93*	*1993-94*	*1994-95*	*1995-96*	*1996-97*	*1997-98*
1.	Target amount	2500	2500	3500	4000	7000	5000	4800
2.	Amount realised	3038	1913	0	4843	361	380	902
3.	% of amount realized from disinvestment to targeted amount	123.5	54.6	0	121	2.4	7.6	18.8
4.	Fiscal deficit	36,325	40,173	60,257	57,704	60,243	56,242	73,204
5.	Disinvestment amount as % of fiscal deficit	8.36	4.76	0	8.39	0.28	0.57	3.04
6.	Capital receipt	38,528	36,178	55,440	68,695	58,338	61,554	83,345
7.	Disinvestment amount as % of capital receipt	7.88	5.28	0	7.05	0.35	0.75	3.09
8.	Internal debt	172,750	199,100	245,712	266,417	307,869	344,476	388,998
9.	Disinvestment amount as % of internal debt	3.76	0.96	0.00	3.82	0.05	0.11	0.23

TABLE 3.22

Contributions of disinvestment proceeds in meeeting fiscal deficit from FY 1998-99 to 2003-04 (Amount in crore)

Sl. No.	*Details*	*1998-99*	*1999-00*	*2000-01*	*2001-02*	*2002-03*	*2003-04*
1.	Target amount	5000	10000	10000	12000	120000	13200
2.	Amount realized	5371	1860	1871	5632	3348	15547
3.	% of amount realized from disinvestment to targeted amount	107.4	15.8	18.71	46.93	27.9	117.78
4.	Fiscal deficit	89560	104717	118816	140955	131306	132103
5.	Disinvestment amount as % of fiscal deficit	5.90	3.98	3.57	4.00	2.55	13.77
6.	Capital receipt	106,276	116,571	132,987	162,500	168,648	184,860

(Contd.)

7.	Disinvestment amount as % of capital receipt	5.14	3.57	3.41	3.47	3.99	8.41
8.	Internal debt	459,696	714,254	803,698	913,061	102,0689	115,8639
9.	Disinvestment amount as % of internal debt	3.17	0.26	0.23	0.62	0.33	3.14

Source: Data for Fiscal Deficit, Internal Debt and Capital Receipt is taken from Govt. of India's Economic Surveys (1996-97 to 2003-04) for various years.

GRAPH 3.1

Receipt and expenditure of the Central Government from 1991-92 to 1997-98

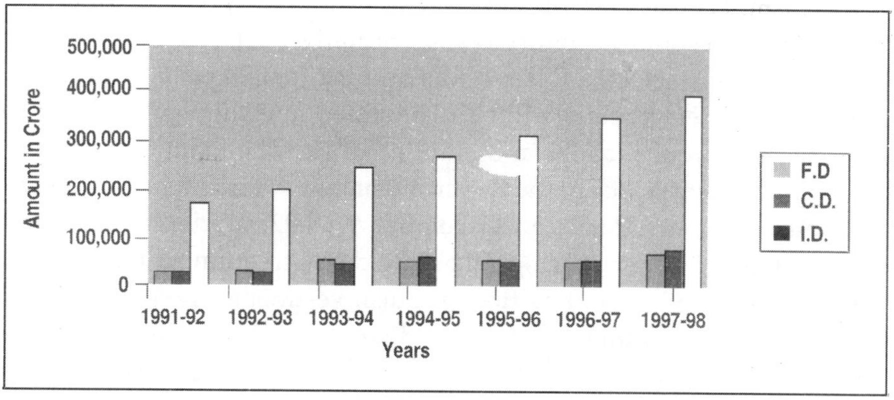

GRAPH 3.2

Receipt and expenditure of the Central Government from 1998-99 to 2003-04

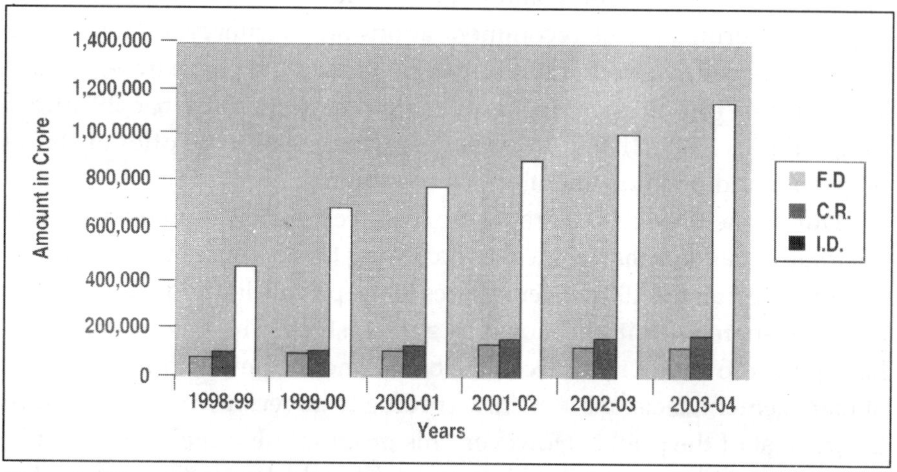

Where F.D. = Fixed Deposit,
I.D. = Internal Debt, and
C.R. = Capital Receipt.

Conclusion

The process of disinvestment means selling off partially or wholly the assets of public sector undertakings to private sector. In India, however, disinvestment came to form part of the government policy in the beginning of the 1990s when a self-proclaimed socialist Chandrasekhar happened to head a short-lived government at the centre. His finance minister Yashwant Sinha, while introducing the budget for 1991-92, proposed to dispose of 20 per cent shares of selected state undertaking to the private sector in order to raise resources to tide over ongoing financial crisis. Before this proposal could be implemented, the Chandrasekhar government fell and his finance minister went to BJP, a professed enemy of socialism. Then in 1991, the P. V. Narsimha Rao Government continued the policy of economic reforms and formally declared the policy of disinvestment in selected PSEs. It was decided that 20 per cent of equity of such public enterprises will be disinvested and they will be sold to financial institutions, banks and employees etc. The main objectives of the disinvestment policy of the Government, as per statement laid in both the houses of parliament on December 9, 2002, modernization and upgradation of PSEs, retiring of public debt, creation of new assets, generation of employment, setting up a disinvestment proceeds fund and formulating the guidelines for the disinvestment of natural assets companies. To achieve these objectives a Disinvestment Commission was set-up in 1996 to carefully examine withdrawal of public sector from non-core, non-strategic areas with assurance to workers of job security or of opportunities for retraining and re-employment. The Commission, in its three-year term, gave its recommendations on 58 enterprises referred to it and proposed, instead of public offerings as in the past, strategic trade sales involving change in ownership/management for 29 and 8 undertakings respectively. In other cases, there was to be offer of shares or closure and postponement of disinvestment.

During the 1999-2000, a proposal of disinvestment was mooted through the issue of Golden share concept. According to this concept, Government will disinvest all the 100 per cent shares to the private individual and retain only one share with itself known as golden share. The golden share will have power to have a nominee in the board and the power to veto all types of management decisions, which, according to government will go against the interest of the public. However, this proposal ultimately could not be implemented because it wanted amendment to the Indian Companies Act, which permits only the issue of equity share and preference share and not golden share. After a lot of deliberation and experiments with different forms of disinvestment, the Department of Disinvestments proposed strategic sale of almost all PSEs in the non-strategic areas to highest bidders who will be allowed to purchase up to 74% of Government equity in the company. Initially the government stake in these PSEs could be brought down to 51% and later on further to 26%. It was imagined that the perception of shareholders value in these PSEs would change automatically once the government reduces its stake to fewer than 51%. In 2002-03, the disinvestment mechanism was broadened to include offer for sales of residual shares in privatized PE's and a minority portion of government equity in select PSEs. There was an initial public offering by Maruti Udyog Ltd. in June 2003, which received an overwhelming response from institutional and retail investors? This was followed by offers for sale of residual shares of privatized PSEs, *viz.*, CMC Ltd., IBP Ltd. and Indian Petro-Chemicals Corporation Ltd., and a portion of government equity in Dredging Corporation of India Ltd., GAIL and ONGC.

Further, there was no coordination between Disinvestment Ministry and concerned ministry in which disinvested PSEs comes. There was a clash between Disinvestment Minister, Arun Shourie and Pramod Mahajan, when the question of disinvesting the equity of HPCL and IPCL came first time in parliament; Arun Shourie was on one side and Petroleum Minister Ram Nayak was on another side. Even on many cases different components of NDA Government were not unanimous on disinvestment of particular PSE. Any plan of disinvestment initiated by Arun Shourie is neither based on cost nor is it backed by efficiency that is why this disinvestments policy faced criticism by different components of NDA Government. Even coordinator of NDA Government, George Fernandez, criticised and rather obstructed the new disinvestment plans of PSEs started by Arun Shourie to be implemented. George Fernadez also raised question on the working of marketing system of two public sector oil refineries.

After the defeat of National Democratic Alliance (NDA) in 14th Lok Sabha elections in 2004, UPA Government came in power and formed the Government. But in continuous pressure of leftist parties the government has closed down the Ministry of Disinvestment and Disinvestment Commission. UPA Government has initiated review of disinvestment of 15 PSEs under the administrative control of the Ministry of Heavy Industries and Public Enterprises. Along with the review of disinvestment cases, the previous government had decided to sell-of, would also be drawn up. Due to these controversies investors/bidders are hesitating to purchase the shares of PSEs offered for strategic sale.

In short, ever since the Ministry of Disinvestment was created, all cases of disinvestment have been of different nature and taught new lessons for refining the procedures. The highlights of the disinvestment completed by the Ministry of Disinvestment so far states that no long-term strategy has been followed in selection of enterprises falling in different industry segments, mostly profitable and of unequal paid-up capital were referred to the disinvestment commission. In individual industry segments, only fertilizers and minerals and metal enterprises were predominantly referred. There were several others enterprises, which were inefficient, loss-making and having low social consideration but were not referred to the commission. The proceeds of disinvestment contribute only a small portion to meet the fiscal deficit and are negligible in retiring internal debt. However, the valuation of shares reveals that enterprises' earlier problem of understanding has been mitigated to a great extent. The criterion for selection of enterprises and the whole process is closely guarded secret.

NOTE

A GDR is a dollar denominated instrument traded on the stock exchanges in Europe or US or both. Usually they represent a certain number of equity shares. Though GDR is denominated in dollars, the underlying shares are denominated in rupees.

REFERENCES

1. Agrawal, P.; Gokran, Subir V.; Mishra Vina; Parikh, K.S. and Sen, Kunal (1996). *Economic Restructuring in East Asia and India — Perspectives on Policy Reform.* Macmillan India Ltd.
2. Attahir, B. Yusuf. *Privatizing State Enterprises: A Strategic Management Perspective,* in Management and Change, Vol. 4, January–June 2000. pp. 209–219.
3. Azam, K.J. (1997). *Sustaining the Economic Reform in India: The Political Economy Constraints,* in Economic Liberalization in India: Implications for Indo-US Relations, Delta Publishing House.
4. Bajpai, Nirupama. *Economic Reforms in Developing Countries: Theory and Evidence,* in Economic and Political Weekly, Vol. XXX, No. 2, January 14, 1995.

5. BASU, JAYA. *Disinvestment — BILT's Paper Dreams,* in Business Today, December 21, 2000, pp. 51-52.
6. BATRA, G.S. AND BHATIA, B.S. *Liberalization in Indian Economy: An Evaluation of Recent Public Sector Reforms and Privatization Strategies,* in The Journal of Institute of Public Enterprises, Vol. 17, No. 1 & 2, Jan.-March, April-June, 1994.
7. CHANDRASEKHAR, C.P. *Murky Side of Privatization,* in People's Democracy, Vol. 25, No. 25, June 2001.
8. CHARLIES, FOMBRUM AND MARK, SHANLY. *What's A Name? Reputation Building and Corporate Strategy,* in Academy of Management Journal, Vol. 33, No. 2, June 1990.
9. DAS, K. DEBENDRA AND VISHNUDEO, BHAGAT (1994). *Economies of Privatization — Issues and Options,* Deep and Deep Publications, New Delhi.
10. DHRYMES, PHOEBUS J. *Socially Responsible Investment: Is It Profitable?* In The Investment Research Guide to Socially Responsible Investing, the Colloquium on Socially Responsible Investing, 1998.
11. DUTTA, AMITAVA K. *Uncertain Success: The Political Economy of Indian Economic Reform,* in Journal of International Affairs, Summer 1997, pp. 57-83.
12. DHAR, P.N. *The Political Economy of Development in India,* Indian Economic Review, Vol. XXII, No. 1 (1987), pp. 1–18.
13. Economy bureau *Govt. Firm on IA, A-I Sell-off This Fiscal,* in Business Standard, New Delhi, November 14, 2000.
14. GUISLAIN, PIERRE. *Divestiture of State Enterprises,* Washington: World Bank Technical Paper:186.
15. http://hindustan.net/discus/messages
16. HEALD, D.A. AND STEEL, D.R. *Privatizing Public Enterprises: Options and Dilemmas,* in Royal Institute of Public Administration, London, 1981.
17. KAUR, SIMIRIT. *Public Enterprises Disinvestment in India — A Theoretical and Empirical Framework,* in The Journal of Institute of Public Enterprises, Vol. 21, No. 1 & 2, Jan.–March, April-June 1998.
18. NAIB, S. (2002). *"Ownership — Does it Matter",* Productivity, **43(2):** 303–313.
19. SANKAR, T.L. AND REDDY, Y.V. (1989). *Privatization: Diversification of Ownership of Public Enterprises,* Hyderabad: Institute of Public Enterprises and Booklinks Corporation.

20. SINGH, HARVINDER (2000). *Performance Evaluation of State Enterprises*, Deep and Deep Publications, New Delhi.
21. VENKITARAMAN, S. *Disinvestment in Public Sector Undertaking*, in Chartered Secretary, Vol. 21, No. 6, June 1991, pp. 469-470.
22. www.divest.nic.in
23. WORLD BANK. *Private Participation in Indian Infrastructure*, World Bank, 1999.

CHAPTER 4

Privatization Policy Framework

Introduction

The first four decades since independence witnessed an impressive growth of Public Sector Enterprises (PSEs) as they were envisaged as a matter of policy to assume the 'commanding heights' of the economy. The generally poor performance of PSEs in relation to expected goals radically altered the perceptions about the role of PSEs in the last decade and a half, and a persistently weak fiscal position brought to the fore the need for reforming the PSEs. Privatization aimed at enhancing competition and efficiency figured prominently in the initiatives launched to reform PSEs—a trend that is commonly observed now in many developing countries and therefore, has become a very vital measure of economic renovation in both developed and developing economies. There are different ways of achieving privatization which have been followed from time to time. It cannot be achieved entirely till certain conditions are not fulfilled.

But is the private sector a complete paragon of virtue? If yes, what should be the modality for privatisation? These are the issues, which have been extensively debated both at the national and international levels. Though the efficacy of privatization is still being debated at the theoretical levels, there is a growing consensus in favour of privatization among policy makers. The present chapter essentially reviews this much talked issue, further reaffirms the broad consensus and analyses the various divesture and non-divesture options for privatization and, besides examining the strategy adopted for privatization, also discusses the conditions without which, the objective of privatization is difficult to achieve.

Strategy for Privatization

Privatization means transfer of ownership and/or management of an enterprise from the public sector to the private sector. It also implies sale or transfer of majority portion of the shares in a public enterprise to a private entity. Another dimension of privatization is opening up of an industry that had been reserved for the public sector to the private sector.

Privatization has been a very important integral part of economic reforms in the erstwhile communist countries. Even non-communist developing economies too have been carrying out privatization in varying forms, degrees and measure of success. In short, privatization has become a very vital measure of economic rejuvenation in both developed and developing economies.

There are different ways of achieving privatization. Each country has its own gimmicks.

- One of the important ways of privatization is divestiture, or privatization of ownership through the sale of equity.
- The second modality is de-nationalization or re-privatization.
- The third modality is the government withdrawing from the provision of certain goods and services, leaving them completely or partly to the private sector.
- The fourth modality is privatization of management, using leases and management contracts.

If privatization is to succeed in the sense of raising efficiency or effectiveness in the production or delivery of goods and services, certain conditions must be satisfied.

This chapter examines these issues and suggests certain measures derived from divestiture experience, which could increase the probability of success of reforms.

Essential Elements of Privatization Strategy

Professor Samuel Paul points out that if privatization/disinvestment is to succeed, the following seven conditions must be met:

First, privatization cannot be sustained unless the political leadership is committed to it, and unless it reflects a shift in preferences of the public, arising out of dissatisfaction with the performance of their alternatives. Privatization has in the past worked best when a government was strongly committed to a change, or when a new government vowed to reverse the actions of its predecessors.

Second, any alternative institutional arrangements chosen should not stifle competition among suppliers. Replacement of a government monopoly by a private monopoly may not increase public welfare; there must be a multiplicity of private supplier.

The *third* related condition is freedom of entry to provide goods and services. Long-term contracts and franchises limit competition and consumers' choice. In some services that are capital intensive, freedom of entry is difficult to achieve. But in others, such as refuse collection or health services, the public will be better served by several private suppliers competing, than by one agency monopolizing the market through a long-term contract.

Fourth, public services to be provided by the private sector must be specific or have measurable outcome.

Fifth, consumers should be able to link the benefits they receive from a service to the costs they pay for it.

Sixth, privately provided services should be less susceptible to fraud than the government services, if they are to be effective.

Seventh, equity is an important consideration in the delivery of public services. Broadly speaking, the benefits of privatization can accrue to the capital owner, who supplies the services to the consumer, who receives a more efficient service; and to the public at large, through a reduction in the public sector deficit; and in taxes or the rate of inflation, or both.

There are several modes of achieving privatization. If a country is ready to reform, according to the nature of market in which they are operating, we classify PSEs into competitive and non-competitive.

The privatization process itself is also easier if the enterprise is in a competitive sector and the environment is market friendly. On the other hand, for the sale of enterprise in non-competitive sectors, the steps are more numerous and the process is more difficult. In order to look into different decisions under different country conditions and enterprise' conditions, a framework for decision-making is given below in Table 4.1.

Criterion for Reform Options

Privatization cannot be achieved unless a country is ready for such a reform. When a government is committed for such a change, it has many options about how to handle each enterprise. The option to choose will depend upon the firm, the nature of the market and the country's capacity to divest.

TABLE 4.1
Framework for decision-making

Country conditions	*Enterprise conditions*	
	Competitive	*Non-competitive*
High capacity to regulate (market-friendly)	Decision • Sell	Decision • Ensure or install appropriate regulatory environment • Then consider sale
Low capacity to regulate (market-unfriendly)	Decision • Sell, with attention to competitive conditions	Decision • Considering privatization of management arrangements • Instal market-friendly policy framework • Instal appropriate regulatory environment • Then consider sale

Source: Privatization: The Lesson of Experience, World Bank Publications (1993 edition), p. 5.

Enterprises in competitive condition must be divested in such a way that competition is enhanced and the sale is transparent. On the other hand, enterprises in non-competitive condition, two issues should be considered:

First, unbundled large firms by say, breaking a national monopoly into regional monopolies or by differentiating one division from the other like electricity generation from distribution.

Second, ensure proper regulation through benchmark regulation or price cap rather than rate of return regulation. This is obvious because rate of regulation does not include the firm to costs.

Criterion for Selection of Enterprises for Privatization

One of the most significant changes in the Indian economic sector over the past decade has been the growth and development of disinvestment in public sector enterprises (PSEs). For the last forty-five years we had been following a path in which the public sector was expected to be the engine of growth. However, from the middle of the seventies, disappointment with the public sector had started, but the voices of protest were very weak and infrequent. The disappointment of public sector to fulfill the role assigned to it strengthened the voices of protest. Even it was realized by the Central Government that PSEs have live longer than the purposes for which they were once established. Therefore, it is better to privatize them before situation become worsen. But what should be the appropriate criterion for selecting an enterprise for privatization is important issue which must be answered to understand the concept of disinvestment crystal clear. Experience suggests that a healthy and competitive PSE can fetch better price in the market in comparison to a sick PSE. But then the question arises about the suitability of further putting money in PSEs, and the capability and the competence of the present management to undertake the restructuring, which they had done before. While a restructured PSE would most likely fetch better price in the market, one should make a cost-benefit analysis to find out the extent of incremental social and financial benefit the Government would receive by selling the restructured units.

1. Comparative advantage criteria

There is nothing wrong in saying that loss-making public sector enterprises should be privatized or closed or sold, if cannot be revived. Ramanadham [1989, 1991(a) and (b)] also advices that when a public sector loses its comparative advantage, it is better to privatize it before huge losses occur.

According to Ramanadham, the comparative advantage is to be measured in terms of the commercial returns, social returns and a desired trade-off between them. As experience suggests that socio-financial return combinations normally are different among different enterprises or sectors, therefore, the concept of comparative advantage should be addressed in an enterprise-specific and time-specific manner.

2. Economic criteria

Jones et al. (1990) have suggested a model to answer which enterprises should be disinvested first? According to them, public asset should be sold only if the seller is better off after the sale, *i.e.*, the change in welfare (ΔW) is positive. If the government behaves as a private seller, then this would merely necessitate that the sale price surpass the value of the future-earning stream foregone, *i.e.*,

Sell public asset if

$$\Delta W = Z - V_{sg} > 0$$

where ΔW = Change in welfare

Z = Price at which the sale is executed

V_{sg} = Social value under continued government option.

As the government is concerned about the overall welfare of the society, it must also consider about the firm's performance after sale (V_{sp}), *i.e.*, social value under private manoeuver. The social value under private manoeuver is the present value of expected net benefits accruing to society as a whole from the private operation of enterprise. However, the government is free to use this proceed to retire some of its own amount overdue, thereby realizing new funds to the private sector and thus could offer the crowding-out effect.

To examine how the sale proceeds are used, depends on the difference between the private and government revenue multipliers. This sales proceed has both a behavioural impact (reflected in the $\lambda_g - \lambda_p$ differential). Considering these parameters, the decision to sell public asset becomes:

Sell if, $$\Delta W = V_{sp} - V_{sg} + (\lambda_g - \lambda_p)Z > 0$$

Reorganizing these variables,

Sell if, $$Z > \frac{V_{sg} - V_{sp}}{\lambda_g - \lambda_p}$$

This implies that whenever social welfare is higher under private ownership than public, the government should not hesitate to sell these public sectors' assets.

Techniques of Privatization

Today, there are numerous techniques of privatization besides strategic sale and public flotation, such as management contract, lease, management/ employee buy-out, trade sale, public auction, mass or voucher privatization and liquidation, followed by sale of assets. While management contracts and leases are non-divestiture options (suitable for hotels in prime locations), the rest are forms of divestiture. Many countries have tried these options with various degrees of success. For example, mass or voucher privatization was the main method of sale in East European countries, as was strategic sale in Sri Lanka, Brazil, Chile, Jamaica and a host of African states. Some countries like UK have opted for more than one form of privatization. In the UK, there have been private placements and employee buy-outs in addition to public flotation. In Poland, privatization through liquidation is the popular mean, particularly with small and medium-size firms. The various techniques for privatizing the public sector throughout the globe are discussed as follows:

1. Public offering of shares

Under this technique, the government sells an enterprise to the general public all or large lock of shares, it holds. For this purpose, a prospectus is prepared for the offering and normally the service of an investment bank, as adviser is required. The offering may be on a fixed price or on a tender basis, and the shares may be marketed internationally or only domestically.

Generally, this technique is used for a profitable, large-scale PSEs, otherwise in case of a weak performing firm, a public offering is made only after its restructuring.

2. Direct private sale

Under this technique, the government sells the shares of a firm directly to private buyers without taking the services of financial intermediaries such as brokers, underwriters or other agencies. This results in lower floatation costs and better speed.

Direct sale may involve the participation of foreign bidders, either as competitive bidders or as selected buyers, who may have been chosen because they possess the necessary capital, technology and know-how.

The foremost advantage of this technique is that the prospective buyer can be known in advance.

3. New private investment in PSEs

This technique is preferable when the government's objective is both to reduce its proportionate shareholding, and the enterprise is short of capital. The distinguish feature of such privatization is that the government is not disposing of any of its existing equity in the PSEs, rather, it increases the equity position and causes a dilution of the government's equity position. The net outcome of this technique will be the joint ownership (private/government) of the company.

4. Management/Employees buy-out

This technique offers advantage in terms of employees/management motivation to find ways to costs and improve productivity. This technique refers to the acquisition of a controlling shareholding in a firm. This option may involve Leveraged Management Buy-Outs (LMBO), wherein purchase is debt-financed and the assets are used as security for it.

5. Joint ventures

A joint venture is where two or more persons (either individual people or companies) enter into an agreement to undertake a business venture for joint profits and risks. This partnership often involves a foreign partner who may provide capital and know-how, for the transfer of some shares in his name. The joint venture can be simply an agreement between the parties as to who does what, invests what and gets what at the end, or it can be an entirely new company set-up for the specific purpose of pursuing the joint business.

6. Liquidation—Sale of PSEs assets

Liquidation has two meanings in finance. The *first* is converting securities into cash. The *second* is the sale of assets of a company to one or more acquirers in order to pay-off debts. Thus, the process of dissolving a business by selling the assets, paying the debts, and distributing the remaining equity to the owners is known as **liquidation**. The government adopts this option when it seems more lucrative to sell assets instead of entire enterprises. This technique of disinvestment is popular in Poland, particularly with small business enterprises.

7. Fragmentation—Re-organization of enterprises

The act of imposing a new organization, organizing differently (often involving extensive and drastic changes) is generally termed as **re-organization**. Under this technique, an organization is broken up into small several parts. It also involves hiving off of some activities. This technique is adopted when an organization is involved in different types of activities, that in cumulative are not lucrative for potential investors. The government may wish to sell only certain components of the PSEs while retaining others. The second reason behind this philosophy may be that due to monopolistic situation of any PSE, now in the welfare of general being, the government is interested in fragmentation of an PSE into component parts to create competition, for instance in electric generation and distribution.

8. Mass privatization

Literally, mass privatization means "the permanent transfer of property rights from the state to the private sector". Typical forms of mass privatization include: sale of shares to private investors, Build-Operate-Own (BOO) models, Management Buy-In (MBI)[1] models, Management Buy-Out (MBO)[2] models, Employee Buy-Out (EBO)[3] models, or voucher systems. Therefore, this is also termed as "coupon or voucher privatization". Generally, this technique is used in the Central and Eastern Europe. The main feature of mass privatization is that it is based on the population-wide distribution of vouchers or certificates free of charge or for a nominal fee. These vouchers are distributed to all adult citizens.

This technique is generally supported because of rapid transfer of ownership from the state to individual shareholders. On the other hand, the main argument against mass privatization is that it does not, in itself, result in improved economic efficiency due to widely dispersed ownership that may result in effective control of the privatized enterprises.

9. Public auctions

By and large, 'public auction' means a gathering at a pre-announced public location to sell property to satisfy a mortgage that is in default, or a sale of an asset through competitive, usually oral bidding. In case of privatization, this technique is used for small or medium sized PSEs, which do not require technology transfers or other special inputs. The main **advantages** of this technique are:

- The process is comparatively fast.
- Transparent technique due to open competitive bidding.
- Cost effective.

This technique is generally used in some parts of Central and Eastern Europe for selling hotels, shops, restaurants and repair workshops.

[NOTE: Experience shows that no single method is successful in all countries, the success or failure of a privatization technique depends on a number of factors such as the state of the stock market, the degree of competition, the liberalisation and economic policies (including the extent of foreign ownership) of the country, and the level of entrepreneurship available in the country.]

In India, the first attempts at disinvestment/privatization were through selling small percentages of shares of both good and not-so-good companies by bundling and offering them to financial institutions. This technique of disinvestment, practised from 1991-92 to 1998-99, was criticised by the then Comptroller and Auditor General (CAG). Then in 2000, the then government opted for strategic sale[4] as the method of disinvestment. After the defeat of National Democratic Alliance (NDA) in 14th Lok Sabha elections, the new coalition government, with left parties supporting the congress decided to follow privatization of loss-making firms on a 'case-by-case' basis after obtaining workers' approval as the Common Minimum Programme (CMP) of the United Progressive Alliance (UPA) is against disinvestment of profitable PSEs.

Conclusion

In India, although there were some isolated cases of privatization, no definite policy decision was taken until the new economic policy has been ushered in.

The new economic policy took some bold steps regarding the restructuring of the public sector. Its **salient features** are:

- Portfolio of public sector investments to be reviewed with a view to focus the public sector on strategic, high-tech and essential infrastructure;
- The sick public sector enterprises will be referred to the Board of Industrial and Financial Reconstruction (BIFR) or other similar institutions for the formulation of revival/rehabilitation schemes;
- A part of the government shareholding in the public sector would be offered to the financial institutions, mutual funds, workers and general public, in order to raise resources and encourage wider public participation.

Regarding choice of enterprises for privatization, an enterprise whose presence in the public sector has no economic justification should be selected automatically for disinvestment. The disinvestment policy involves that the well known and best-run enterprises should be divested first, as buyers are easily available. In case foreign buyers are involved, proper care should be taken to structure the transaction in a way that there are no undue gains to foreigners at the cost of domestic buyers.

In countries where there are well functioning capital markets, disinvestment entails selling stock to the public. In industrial countries, privatization has come mainly through divestiture of the government economic activities. The developing countries like Brazil, Bangladesh and Pakistan are also present examples of disinvestment.

While formulating privatization strategy, one should not ignore the concerns of employees, workers and consumers. Disinvestment policies should be practical and customized to the specific state of affairs and uniqueness of the nation concerned. To conclude, we can say, while making and implementing disinvestment programme/policies, social, economic, institutional and political risks should be cautiously analyzed.

Further, transfer of pan of shares to the public financial institutions does not represent true privatization, unless the privatization of a unit is not substantial, it is not going to be meaningful.

NOTES

1. The purchase of a large, and often controlling, interest in a company by an investor group who wishes to retain existing management.
2. A management buyout (MBO) occurs when a company's managers buy or acquire a large part for which they work from their employing company. A management buyout most generally occurs when the business is under threat of closure and the existing management team believes that they can save it. It carries high risks but, if successful, the rewards can be very great.
3. In an employee buyout (EBO), management and a broad group of employees complete a transaction which result in an enterprise being more than 50% owned by its employees, or a "majority employee owned enterprise". Management is included, but the buyout is not limited to management and investors. Investors are often needed and included when a change of control (majority) buyout is necessary or desired.
4. Strategic sale implies selling of a substantial block of government holdings to a single party, which would not only acquire substantial equity holdings of up to 51 per cent but also bring in the necessary technology for making the public sector enterprise viable and competitive in the global market.

REFERENCES

1. BASU, P.K. *Performance Evaluation for Performance Improvement — An Essay on the Strategies Management of Public Enterprises in India,* Allied Publishers, New Delhi.
2. BERG, E. AND SHIRLEY, M.M. *Divestiture in Developing Countries,* in Papers of Workshop on Foreign Investment and Divestiture: The Gambia, October 17–28, 1989. New York, UN, 1998.
3. BOS, D. *A Theory of the Privatization of the Public Enterprises,* in Journal of Economics, Supplementum 5, 1986.
4. CHAKRAVARTY, S.R. *Efficient Horizontals Mergers,* in Journal of Economic Theory, Vol. 82, No. 1, September 1998.
5. DUTT RUDDAR. (ed.) (1993). *Privatization—Bane or Panacea,* Pragati, New Delhi.
6. GURU, D.D.; GOPAL SINGH, B. AND SINGH, A.K. *Rapporteuer's Reports: Globalization of Indian Economy,* Economic Thought of Mahadev Govind Ranade—Economics of Privatization, in The Indian Economic Journal, Vol. 41, No. 2, Oct.–Dec. 1993.
7. M. L. R. ENTERPRISES INC. *The Pros and Cons of the Split-off,* in Mergers and Acquisitions, Jan.-Feb. 12, 1995.
8. MAITRA, DILIP AND MAZUMDAR, RAKHI. *Merger and Acquisitions — Will Mindales Roll in India?* In Business Today, April 7–21, 2000, pp. 34-35.
9. NARULA, MANOJ. *An Indian Divestment Increases Credibility,* in Business India, May 29–June 11, 2000.
10. OBAIDULLAH, MD. *Privatization Through Disinvestment,* in Chartered Accountant, Vol. 38, No. 9, March 1990, pp. 681–683.
11. RAMAMURTI, R. *Why are Developing Countries Privatizing?* in Journal of International Business Studies, Vol. 23, No. 2, 1992, pp. 225–249.
12. RAO, S.L. *Public Enterprises Reform,* in The Indian Economic Journal Vol. 41, No. 2, Oct.–Dec. 1993.
13. RUDRA, ASHOK. *Privatization and Deregulation,* in Economic and Political Weekly, Vol. XXXVI, No. 51, December 1991.
14. SRINIVASAN, T.N. *Privatization and Deregulation,* in Economic and Political Weekly, 27, (15 & 16), April 1992, pp. 843–848.

CHAPTER 5

Ownership Vs Competition

Public Interest Theory and Market Failure

The public interest theory of regulation explains that regulation seeks the protection and benefit of the public at large. This theory of economic regulation is rooted in perception that government must step in to regulate markets in instances when markets are unable to regulate themselves. These so-called 'market failures' occur where the price mechanism that regulates supply and demand breaks down, forcing government to take action. Natural monopolies and external costs are the most common types of market failure. Natural monopolies occur when the fixed costs of supplying a good are so great that it makes sense for only one company to supply that good. Public utilities like the delivery of electricity or water/wastewater services to your home usually require so much money to build the necessary infrastructure that no company would take on the task without confidence that it would control a sizeable portion of the market.

The results of the empirical work also support that the problem is the monopoly businesses that arise from this situation tend to use their market power in ways that can be highly detrimental to the community at large. This is where governmental regulation becomes important. Externalities occur when the costs or benefits of producing a good or service are not fully included into the price. For instance, economists often cite air pollution as a cost incurred by almost any sort of economic activity, but is often ignored when determining the prices. When the polluting activity is very concentrated, as in a manufacturing plant, the costs to the surrounding community can be considerable. Yet, without governmental regulation there is nothing that compels the plant to either minimize the environmental impact or otherwise compensate the community for bearing that part of the cost of production. These sorts of market failures, along with the general need for mechanisms of regular public disclosure by business, make regulation critical if the public interest is to be protected.

Hypothetical Viewpoints on the Effects of Ownership

What matters ownership or competition?

Public interest theory of regulation explains government intervention in markets and associated regulatory rules as responses to market failures and market imperfections. This theory argues that regulation promotes the general welfare rather than the interests of well-organized stakeholders. The main objective for setting up the public sector as stated in the Industrial Policy Resolution of 1956 is to help in the rapid economic growth and industrialization of the country and create the necessary infrastructure for economic development. Whereas for private sector, it is to earn profit and multiply the investment made. This leads to the *public interest theory* of public sector enterprise. According to this theory, it has been observed throughout the globe for decades that wherever private sector is in the main lead of business, it automatically increases the overall performance of the public sector. This is due to principle of survival which makes public sector employees to work hard if they have to survive and are interested to maintain their identity in whatever business they are.

However, the public interest theory does not consider the 'agency problem' of both the sectors. The ownership of both these sectors face a similar 'agency problem', that is, how executives and other employees should be encouraged so that to achieve optimum capacity utilization of the personnel so as to contribute maximum to the owners' objectives.

In this regard, it is relevant to understand that competition among enterprises is a tool to solve the enterprise 'agency problem' in a number of ways:

Firstly, the competition establishes direct links between the performance and rewards of the management. Competitive markets provide the best means of ensuring that the economy's resources are put to their best use by encouraging enterprise and efficiency, and widening choice.

Secondly, it generates information that is valuable to the owners of enterprises.

Lastly, where private sector works well, it provides strong incentives for good performance—encourage public sector to improve productivity, to reduce prices and to innovate; whilst rewarding consumers with lower prices, higher quality, and wider choice.

Therefore, it has rightly been observed and said that ownership is not the only determinant of incentive structure and factors like competitive conditions in the market. The key hypothesis pertaining to the 'agency problem' at the enterprise level is the ownership associated with a more effective incentive structure than public ownership. Therefore, there will be less scope for personnel (both for executives and workers) in private ownership to pursue their own objectives at the expense of owners. The key weapon that keeps a private company on tenterhooks is *survival.* There are private companies that are as mismanaged as public companies, but that does not last long. They shut down, get bought over, or gird up their loins when faced with looming fate.

On the other side, the public sector ownership is not free from criticism. A general criticism of public ownership is that the monitoring of these enterprises is very poor and the 'principal agent problem' exists much more severe than that in private sector. This causes a lot of problems, as monitoring is done by civil servants, voters' elected political nominees and the managers of public sector, who are not the experts of the concerned field. A bureaucrat always could not be supposed to be a policy maker of economic affairs. Unfortunately, they are both the policy makers and the implementers in our country and are making policies for their loaves and fishes. Thus, the political and bureaucratic intervention in day-to-day functioning of the public sector leads to a number of 'principal agent problems'.

Therefore, to rectify these problems, bureaucrats and/or politicians responsible for monitoring PSEs should themselves be viewed as agents of the public and the welfare of public should be their ultimate responsibility.

Relative Performance of Public and Private Firms in Global Context

Disinvestment today is not only a vehicle to bridge budgetary gaps but has become an integral part of corporate restructuring. Disinvestment as a concept was first taken up energetically in the UK and USA from where it spread to rest of the countries, and has since become a global phenomenon. UK and USA are being taken as a landmark because they are the pioneer in disinvestment. Therefore, it is useful to look into the literature and experience of UK and USA (besides India) in this respect to reach at a fair conclusion.

A survey of available literature

In order to study the comparison between public and private sector Trivedi (1990), took six public sector and eight private sector cement companies in India over the period of 1977-78 to 1981-82 after making several adjustments to the sample data to arrive at conclusion. Since financial profitability is neither a necessary nor a sufficient condition for the enhancement of society's well being, he found that as such there is no significant difference between the performance of public and private cement companies over the five years period 1977-78 to 1981-82.

On the basis of the evidence available over the period 1981-82 and 1985-86, Bhaya (1990), concluded that despite higher wages, administered prices and fixed capital, where the public sector management has no control, efficiency of the public sector is not less than the private sector in any way. On the contrary, Jha and Sahni (1992), in order to compare the performance of enterprises under private and public ownership, took four industries: cement, cotton, textiles, electricity and iron & steel. On the basis of ASI data concluded that both the sectors are equally efficient.

In the year 1994, Joshi and Little in order to estimate the real rates of return to investment in the both (public and private) sectors took rates of return as estimate for the public sector and for the organized manufacturing sector (public and private separately) for the period 1960-61 to 1975-76 and 1976-77 to 1986-87 as shown in the Table 5.1.

TABLE 5.1
Real return to investment in case of both public and private sectors

	1960-61 to 1975-76			*1976-77 to 1986-87*		
	Public sector	*Manufacturing*		*Public sector*	*Manufacturing*	
		Public	*Private*		*Public*	*Private*
r_1	5.4	2.1	11.1	6.2	5.2	22.6
r_2	4.0	0.1	7.7	3.3	3.1	16.7

Source: Joshi and Little (1994).

The rate of return r_1[1] is calculated under the assumption that there has been no improvement in the quality of labour, while r_2[2] is based on the assumption that improvement in the quality of labour is measured by the increase in the real wage rate, concluded that private firms are more efficient.

On the data of 1987-88, Sharma and Sinha (1995), based used a 'Cobb-Douglas production function' to study productive efficiency, which combines both technical and allocative efficiencies for the cement industry in India, concluded that public enterprises are not inherently less efficient than the private enterprises. Majumdar (1995), in order to evaluate relative performance difference took government-owned joint sector and private sectors of Indian industry and concluded that private sector firms are more efficient. In another study, Kaur (1998) when compared TFPI[3] of fifteen public and fifteen private enterprises from diverse sectors for the period 1988-89 to 1994-95 and found no relative performance difference between both public and private sectors. In a similar study, recently Naib, S. (2002) compared efficiency of twenty-six enterprises (thirteen public and thirteen private) for a twelve year period from 1988-89 to 1999-2000 and concluded that both public and private firms experienced modest positive annual growth rate during this period.

In order to assess relative cost efficiencies in electricity, Meyer (1975), randomly took thirty public and thirty private companies and collected data for three years—1967, 1968 and 1969, from the statistics of electric utilities in the United States. He concluded that public firms are more efficient. In his research work Neuberg (1977) involved ninety private and seventy-five municipal firms for the year 1972. For this purpose, he used 'Cobb-Douglas cost function' and found that public firms are more efficient than their private counterparts. Similarly, in order to assess whether significant cost differential arises from different behavioural objectives under different modes of ownership, Pescatrice and Trapani (1980), used 'translog cost function' and concluded that comparatively public firms are more efficient than private electric utilities. In a similar study, in order to study the relative performance of public and private electric utilities, Fare, Grosskopf and Logan (1985), concluded that as such there is no significant difference in overall efficiency between both the public and private utilities.

Crain and Zard Koohi (1978) examined twenty-four private and eighty-eight public firms on 1970 cost figures. Their finding was that the public firms are more efficient than their private counterparts. The results also showed that private firms had twenty-five per cent lower costs than the public firms. On the other hand, Bruggink (1982) used a 'Cobb-Douglas cost function' and found private firms are less efficient than the public firms. In a similar study, Feigenbaum and Teeples (1983) took fifty-seven private and two hundred and sixty-two government water companies and concluded that there is no significant difference between the efficiency of public and private sectors.

Pryke (1982), in order to compare economic performance took three industries—airlines, services and hovercraft and the sale of gas and electricity appliances. After analyzing a range of profitability, productivity and output variables, he concluded that in each case, private firms are more efficient. In another study, Vickers and Yarrow (1988) compared profitability of public and private industrial firms from 1970 to 1985 and concluded that private firms are more efficient than public firms. Boardman and Vining (1989) compared the performance of PCs, PSEs and MEs among the five hundred largest non-US industrial firms, and concluded that private ownership is more superior to the similar public firms. In a later study, Boardman and Vining (1992), studied the five hundred largest non-financial corporations in Canada. For this purpose, they characterized ownership in the four following ways—State-owned enterprises; mixed enterprises; cooperatives and private companies. This time again, they concluded that private companies are more efficient than any other form of ownership.

The Centre for Monitoring Indian Economy (CMIE) Pvt. Ltd. which was established in 1976 by the eminent economist Dr. Narottam Shah, monitors the Indian economy and compares the financial performance of public and private sector companies in the different sectors of the economy. Its analysis from FY 1991 to FY 1997 with regard to manufacturing sector reveals that profitability in the public manufacturing sector is comparatively less than the private manufacturing sector as shown in Table 5.2, on the other hand, Table 5.3 shows the comparison between public and private sectors in terms of percentage (%) change under four different heads like PBDIT, PAT etc.

TABLE 5.2
Comparison of profitability: Public and private sectors

Ratio	*1991*	*1992*	*1993*	*1994*	*1995*	*1996*	*1997*
Operating profit/Gross sale							
Total	6.2	5.8	6.7	7.5	7.5	6.0	6.1
Central govt	2.6	2.8	3.4	3.9	4.3	3.2	3.9
Private	8.0	7.3	8.1	9.0	8.8	7.2	7.0
PBDIT/Gross sale							
Total	12.4	12.1	12.5	13.0	13.3	12.4	12.3
Central govt.	9.6	9.5	9.2	9.0	9.2	8.4	8.7
Private	13.8	13.4	13.9	14.7	14.9	14.1	13.9
PAT/Gross sale							
Total	1.8	1.3	2.4	4.4	4.1	2.2	1.8
Central govt.	–0.3	–0.7	–0.7	0.9	1.1	0.2	0.1
Private	3.0	2.3	3.8	5.4	5.2	3.1	2.5

(Contd.)

PAT/Gross fixed assets							
Total	3.9	2.7	4.7	8.2	8.2	4.2	3.0
Central govt.	–0.7	–1.2	–1.3	1.7	2.2	0.4	0.2
Private	6.8	4.9	7.8	11.0	10.6	5.5	4.0
PAT/Net worth							
Total	8.7	5.9	9.4	13.7	12.7	6.7	5.3
Central govt.	–1.6	–3.5	–3.8	4.9	6.0	1.2	0.7
Private	14.7	10.0	13.4	15.7	13.9	7.7	6.1
PAT/Capital employed							
Total	3.5	2.4	4.2	6.8	6.8	3.5	2.6
Central govt.	–0.6	–1.2	–1.3	1.8	2.4	0.5	0.3
Private	6.4	4.4	6.6	8.5	8.0	4.3	3.2
PAT/Total assets							
Total	2.0	1.4	2.5	4.2	4.2	2.2	1.6
Central govt.	–0.3	–0.6	–0.6	0.9	1.2	0.2	0.1
Private	3.8	2.7	4.1	5.5	5.2	2.9	2.2

Source: Corporate Sector, CMIE, May 1999.

TABLE 5.3

A comparison between public and private sectors in terms of some profit retios

	Units	*1999-00*	*2000-01*	*2001-02*	*2002-03*
PBDIT	% change	9.7	9.3	2.0	20.8
Public sector	% change	–0.1	8.1	5.6	59.4
Private sector	% change	12.0	9.6	1.3	12.6
PAT(Profit after tax)	% change	12.0	18.5	–52.1	247.8
Public sector	% change	–	–	–	–
Private sector	% change	20.7	7.4	–24.2	79.1
PBDIT/Sales	Per cent	10.9	10.2	10.3	11.4
Public sector	Per cent	5.9	5.2	5.5	7.8
Private sector	Per cent	13.3	12.7	12.6	13.3
PAT/Sales	Per cent	0.9	1.0	0.5	2.4
Public sector	Per cent	–1.1	–0.6	–1.5	1.3
Private sector	Per cent	1.8	1.8	1.5	2.9

Source: www.cmie.com

Table 5.4 shows the employment in public and organized private sectors. While Table 5.5 shows the comparison between the employees working in public and private sector (both males and females) irrespective of the size of employment including non-agricultural establishments in the private sector employing ten or more employees.

TABLE 5.4
Employment in organised public and private sectors

Year	*Public sector (end-March)*	*Private sector (end-March)*	*Number of persons on the live register (end-December)*
1970-71	11.10	6.73	5.10
1971-72	11.69	6.96	6.90
1972-73	12.40	6.72	8.22
1973-74	12.73	6.75	8.43
1774-75	13.13	6.79	9.33
1975-76	13.63	6.79	9.78
1976-77	14.18	6.95	10.92
1977-78	14.73	7.11	12.68
1978-79	15.58	7.23	14.33
1979-80	15.12	7.24	16.20
1980-81	15.48	7.40	17.84
1981-82	16.28	7.53	19.75
1982-83	16.75	7.39	21.95
1983-84	17.22	7.36	23.55
1984-85	17.58	7.43	26.27
1985-86	17.68	7.37	30.13
1986-87	18.24	7.39	30.25
1987-88	18.32	7.39	30.05
1988-89	18.51	7.45	32.78
1989-90	18.77	7.58	34.63
1990-91	19.06	7.68	36.30
1991-92	19.21	7.85	36.76
1992-93	19.33	7.85	36.28
1993-94	19.45	7.93	36.69
1994-95	19.47	8.06	36.74
1995-96	19.43	8.51	37.43
1996-97	19.56	8.69	39.14
1997-98	19.42	8.75	40.09
1998-99	19.41	8.70	40.37
1999-00	19.31	8.65	41.34
2000-01	19.14	8.65	42.00
2001-02	18.77	8.43	41.17
2002-03	–	–	41.39

Source: Directorate General of Employment and Training, Ministry of Labour, Government of India.

TABLE 5.5
Estimates of employment in organized public and private sectors

(Lakh persons as on March 31)

Years	*Public sector*			*Private sector*			*Public & Private sectors (Total)*		
	Male	*Female*	*Total*	*Male*	*Female*	*Total*	*Male*	*Female*	*Total*
1990	165.22	22.50	187.72	61.88	13.94	75.82	36.44	36.44	263.53
1991	167.10	23.47	190.57	62.42	14.34	76.76	37.81	37.81	267.33
1992	167.81	24.29	192.10	63.67	14.79	78.46	39.08	39.08	270.56
1993	168.49	24.77	193.26	63.01	15.50	78.51	40.26	40.26	271.77
1994	168.80	25.65	194.45	63.41	15.89	79.30	41.54	41.54	273.75
1995	168.66	26.00	194.66	64.31	16.28	80.59	42.28	42.28	275.25
1996	167.94	26.35	194.29	67.20	17.92	85.12	44.26	44.26	279.41
1997	168.31	27.28	195.59	67.77	19.09	86.86	46.37	46.37	282.45
1998	166.55	27.63	194.18	67.37	20.11	87.48	47.74	47.74	281.66
1999	166.04	28.11	194.15	66.80	20.18	86.98	48.29	48.29	281.13
2000	164.57	28.57	193.14	65.80	20.66	86.46	49.23	49.23	279.60
2001	162.79	28.59	191.38	65.62	20.90	86.52	49.49	49.49	277.89
2002	158.86	28.87	187.73	63.83	20.49	84.32	49.35	49.35	272.06

Source: Ministry of Labour (DGE & T).

Notes: (i) Includes all establishments in the public sector irrespective of size of employment and non-agricultural establishments in the private sector employing 10 or more persons.

(ii) Excludes Sikkim, Arunachal Pradesh, Dadra & Nagra Haveli and Lakshadweep as these are not yet covered under the programme.

In this regard, Table 5.6 gives a brief summary of the empirical results on relative efficiency of public and private firms in global context. This table clearly reveals that since 1982, no research work has concluded that the efficiency of public firms is superior as comparison to private enterprises operating in the same business line, while some studies have shown no difference in the efficiency.

TABLE 5.6
Results on relative efficiency of public and private sector enterprises

Sl. No.	*Sectors*	*Public firms are more efficient*	*No significance difference*	*Private firms are more efficient*
1.	Electric Utilities	Meyer (1975), Neuberg (1997), Pescatrice & Trapani (1980)	Fare, Grosskopf and Logan (1985), Atkinson and Halvorsen (1986)	Moore (1970), Peltzman (1971), Pe Aless (1977)
2.	Water	Bruggink (1982)	Feigenbaum and Teeples (1983)	Crain and Zard Koohi (1978)

(Contd.)

3.	Miscellaneous Industries		Bhaya (1990), Trivadi (1990), Jha & Sahni (1992), Sharma & Sinha (1995), Kaur (1998), Naib (2000)	Rowley & Yarrow (1981), Pryke (1982), Boardman & Vining (1989,1992), Joshi & Little (1994), Majumdar (1985)

Source: Compiled by author.

Summary

It is a general opinion that public enterprises stand for less efficient enterprises. Further, objectives of public enterprise are likely to include certain social obligations like welfare maximization rather than the profit maximization. This is also supported by notional prediction of the 'private right theory', which suggests that public firms generally perform less efficient and less profitable than their private counterparts.

On the basis of available empirical evidence on performance of public and private firms, we can conclude that:

(i) There is no substantial difference in the efficiency of both the public and private firms when market situation is significant, as in the case of monopolistic situation of electric utilities and water.

(ii) Whatever the reason may be, in case of competitive market environment, private sector perform more efficiently than their public counterparts.

(iii) In case of deregulated market environment, the matter of survival prevails. Therefore, the performance of both the public and private enterprises improves. This is due to the competition which here acts as driving force and results in the improvement of performance.

(iv) Empirical evidence relating to the hypothesis that public ownership and competition are determinants of firms' productivity. It concludes that public ownership has a significant negative effect on productivity and also that privatisation has a positive impact on efficiency. Furthermore, increased competition is found to have a positive effect on productivity. Therefore, privatization is effective as a means of increasing firms' efficiency, at least in a non-regulated and relatively competitive sector, such as manufacturing.

(v) Efficiency may also be achieved by changing the quality of management and not only by changing the ownership.

NOTES

1. r_1 is estimated as : $r_1 = Gy - (GL \times WL/Y) \div I/Y$
2. r_2 is estimated as : $r_2 = Gy - (GLA \times WL/Y) \div I/Y$
3. TFPI stands for Total Factor Productivity Index.

REFERENCES

1. AGRAWAL, P.; GOKRAN, S.; MISHRA V.; PARIKH K. AND SEN K. (1995). *Economic Restructuring in East Asia and India—Perspectives on Policy Reforms.* MacMillan India Ltd.
2. AHARANI, Y. *The Evolution of Management of State-Owned Enterprises,* Cambridge Mass: Balling.
3. AHEMD, Z.U. et al. *Government Malpractices,* in Report of the Task Forces on Bangladesh Development Strategies for 1990s, Vol. 2, Dhaka, University Press Limited (UPL), pp. 389–407, 1992.
4. FLUNK, Z. LYNCH. *Why Do Firms Merge and Then Divest? A Theory of Financial Synergy,* in Journal of Business, July 1999.
5. GOPINATH, MOHAN. *The Importance of Central Bank Controls in a Liberalized Economy,* in The Journal of Institute of Public Enterprises, Vol. 17, No. 1 & 2, Jan.–March, April–June, 1994.
6. Government of India, Ministry of Finance, Department of Economic Affairs, in Economic Survey, Annual for various years.
7. HAJDI, P.D. *Issues in Globalization,* Yojana, Vol. 38, No. 14 & 15, August 15, 1994.
8. http://texaspolitics.laits.utexas.edu/html/bur/features/0403_02/slide2.html
9. JOSHI AND LITTLE (1994). *India: Macroeconomics and Political Economy,* OUP.
10. NAIB, SUDHIR (2004). *Disinvestment in India: Policies, Procedures, Practices,* Sage Publications, New Delhi.
11. PRASAD, SMAHI. *Maruti Disinvestment at Right Time,* in Business Standard, New Delhi, November 7, 2000.
12. *Procedures for Disinvestment and Constitution of Disinvestment Commission,* Press Information Bureau, August 1, 1996.
13. *PSU Disinvestment: A Smooth One,* in Dalal Street Journal, Vol. 7, No. 6, March 23 –April 5, 1992, pp. 18–19.
14. SARAJA, S. *Privatization or Liberalization —Strategic Options for LDCs,* in Indian Journal of Public Administration, Vol. 37, No. 4, October–December 1991, pp. 677–686.
15. TANDON, K.K. AND TANDON, B.B. (1995). *Indian Economy,* Tata McGraw Hill.

CHAPTER 6

Changes and Impacts on Industry Structure and Operations

Introduction

Disinvestment has been accepted in all kinds of countries, whether poor or rich, developing or developed, leftist or rightist. It is also accepted by all kinds of regimes as an economic necessity, which is being carried out in all kinds of public enterprises, whether big or small, healthy or sick. If we talk of disinvestment in general, it is not just an economic compulsion, but it is a part of the restructuring programme and no country can ignore the social, legal, political and ideological dimensions of disinvestment. In India, compared to Eastern Europe, there has not been much discussion regarding the distribution of shares in the divestiture process. However, disinvestment is regarded as a political issue rather than the economic programme.

The benefits of disinvestment do not lie only in setting targets year after year, but is judged by its contribution to economic effectiveness. The issue of performance of disinvested enterprises through pragmatic evidence has been studied in detail in this chapter. In order to know whether the goal with which disinvestment drive in India started has achieved or not is studied by considering the impact of extent of disinvestment on the financial and operational performance.

Hypothetical Viewpoint on the Performance of Disinvested Companies

One of the most significant changes in the Indian economic sector over the past decade has been the growth and development of disinvestment in public sector enterprises (PSEs). For the last forty-five years we have been following a path in which the public sector was expected to be the engine of growth. However, from the middle of the seventies, disappointment with the public sector had started, but the voices of protest were very weak and infrequent. The disappointment of public sector to fulfill the role assigned to it strengthened the voices of protest. Even it was realized by the Central Government that PSEs have live longer than the purposes for which they were once established. Considering this, the opening of certain sectors earlier reserved for the public sector was undertaken in the beginning of eighties but the government was to some extent hesitant to make a clear statement until 1991 economic policy.

But today, disinvestment being an economic necessity has been carried out all over the world by all kinds of governments whether democratic or totalitarian policy has become an instrument of transferring public property to private hands for the national interest and the industrial economy of the country in particular. The general consensus is that these programmes of corporate restructuring have been highly victorious and therefore desirable to follow.

Indian Disinvestment Programme: Economic Implications

The process of disinvestment of government shareholding in PSEs was initiated with the announcement of New Industrial Policy (1991). It started the process of full scale liberalization and intensified the process of integration of India with global economy. The underlying purpose of the policy was to raise resources, encourage wider public participation and to improve the management efficiency. However, 1991 to 1999 the government had primarily sold minority shares in PSEs. The disinvestment process, however, was accelerated after the department of disinvestment was set-up on 10th December 1999 with the responsibility to deal with all matters relating to disinvestment of central government equity from central PSEs. With the setting up of the department of disinvestment, the strategic sale of PSEs with transfer of management control commenced. Since the beginning of disinvestment in 1991-92, a total amount of 49,214 crore have been realized till FY 2005-06. The yearwise detail of disinvestment is given in Appendix 'A' at the end of the text.

The general expectations to start disinvestment drive in a nation are:

1. Board of public sector companies would be made more professional.
2. It will result in decreased proportion of debt in the capital structure because of the state's withdrawal of debt guarantees and increase in enterprises cost of borrowing.
3. Management of public sector would be granted more autonomy and it would also be held accountable.

4. The sale of PSEs to private hands will result in increased profitability and operating efficiency through reduced employment level.
5. Transfer of public equity in private hands will increase dividend payouts as private investors would demand dividends.

In a review of available empirical evidence on this issue in India, Bhaya (1990) concluded that there appeared to be no systematic difference in the efficiency of public and private sectors. Further, Trivedi (1990), Jha and Sahni (1992), Sharma and Sinha (1995), Kaur (1998), Naib (2000) all conclude that there is as such no difference in the efficiency of the public and private sectors, while Joshi and Little (1994) and Majumdar (1995) suggest an edge for the private sector but the results vary considerably across sectors. Therefore, the findings of the available empirical evidence are not so much informative as many studies focus almost exclusively upon the ownership variable and fail to take proper account of the effects on performance of differences in market structure, regulation, technology upgradation, government interference, overall improvement of the industry profit etc.

In this research work besides examining the efficiency of disinvested PSEs in its totality and under degree of disinvestment, attempt has been made to see the performance difference from various types of industries particularly from competitive and monopoly environment. In order to examine whether the envisaged goal of disinvestment was attained or not, there is a need to study the impact of disinvestment on financial and operational performance of these disinvested PSEs.

Impact of Disinvestment on Financial and Operational Performance

Extent of disinvestment and performance

Methodology

Disinvestment was supposed to be the tool in the hands of government to improve the profitability and functioning of public sector enterprises and also to raise funds to mitigate the fiscal deficits. For the purpose of examining whether the extent of disinvestment makes a difference in the performance of an enterprise, the forty-seven disinvested public sector enterprises were divided in five groups based on percentage disinvested. The groups were — disinvestment made up to < 10 per cent, 10 to 20 per cent, 20 to 30 per cent, 30 to 40 per cent and >40 per cent. The details of these public enterprises are given in Table 6.2. The analysis of this table shows that the level of performance does not depend on the extent of disinvestment but is dependent on the managerial policies and procedures of a particular enterprise, which makes a difference.

TABLE 6.1
Details of enterprises—Percentagewise

Sl. No.	*Disinvestment in per cent (%)*	*Number of PSEs*	*Name of the PSEs*
1.	< 10%	17	AY, CRL, DCI, EIL, FACT, HCabL, HCopperL, HMT, HPF, NTPC, KIOCL, MMTC, NFL, NMDC, NLC, RCFL, ICI
2.	10 to 20%	5	IOC, MRL, SCI, SAIL, NALCO
3.	20 to 30%	5	BRPL, Maruti, ITI, ONGC, BEL
4.	30 to 40%	4	BEML, BHEL, BPCL, CONCOR
5.	> 40%	16	BALCO, GAIL, CMC, HOCL, HPCL, HTL, HZL, IBP, IPCL, MTNL, MFIL, PPL, VSNL, Jessop & Ltd., ITDC, STC

The disinvested public sector enterprises (PSEs) are from various types of industries particularly from competitive and monopoly environment. Since 1991, the public sector enterprises have been disinvested to varying degrees over a period of time. The details of these enterprises under both the environment (competitive and monopoly) is given as follows:

TABLE 6.2
Details of enterprises—Groupwise

Sl. No.	*Total number of PSEs*	*Details of the PSEs**
1.	47	AY, BRPL, BEML, BEL, BHEL, BPCL, BALCO, CRL, CONCOR, CMC, DCI, EIL, FACT, GAIL, Hind Cable, Hind Copper, HMT, HPF, HOCL, HPCL, HTL, HZL, ICI, IOC, ITI, IBP, IPCL, ITDC, Jessop & Ltd., KIOCL, MMTC, MUL, MTNL, MFIL, MRL, NFL, NALCO, NTPC, NMDC, NLC, ONGC, PPL, RCFL, SCI, SAIL, STC, VSNL
2.	29 (PSEs in competitive environment	AY, BEL, DCI, EIL, FACT, HCabL, HCopperL, HMT, HPF, KIOCL, MMTC, NFL, RCFL, ICI, Maruti, ITI, BEML, BHEL, HOCL, Jessop & Ltd., ITDC, STC, SCI, SAIL, NALCO, IPCL, CMC, HZL, MFIL
3.	18 (PSEs in monopoly environment)	CRL, NMDC, NLC, IOC, MRL, BRPL, ONGC, BPCL, CONCOR, BALCO, GAIL, HPCL, HTL, IBP, MTNL, PPL, NTPC, VSNL

*Full details of these PSEs are given in Appendix 'A'.

TABLE 6.3

Comparison of performance change in profitability following disinvestment of PSEs operating in both competitive and monopoly environment

Profitability Factor	*No. of PSEs*	*Mean before*	*Mean after*	*Change in mean (after - before)*	*t-value*
Return on Sales					
Competitive: PBDIT/Sales	29	0.2987	0.1742	–0.1245	–2.9874*
Monopoly: PBDIT/Sales	18	0.3887	0.3416	–0.0471	–1.1923
Competitive: PAT/Sales	29	0.0819	–0.1714	–0.2533	–1.1964
Monopoly : PAT/Sales	18	0.2314	0.2649	0.0155	0.2776
Return on Assets					
Competitive: PBDIT/Assets	29	0.2186	0.1776	–0.0410	–1.9821
Monopoly : PBDIT/Assets	18	0.3117	0.3218	–0.0101	–0.5728
Competitive: PAT/Assets	29	0.0932	0.0599	–0.0333	–1.8426
Monopoly : PAT/Assets	18	0.1423	0.1628	0.0205	2.4631*
Return on Equity					
Competitive: PBDIT/Equity	29	0.4163	0.2986	–0.1177	–3.004*
Monopoly : PBDIT/Equity	18	0.5145	0.4107	–0.1038	–1.8429
Competitive: PAT/Equity	29	0.0998	0.0219	–0.0779	–2.9131*
Monopoly : PAT/Equity	18	0.2189	0.2134	–0.0055	–0.2158

*Found statistically significant.

Performance of disinvested PSEs under competitive environment

Under the competitive environment, the profitability ratios of 29 enterprises were examined in terms of ROS, ROA, and ROE. It was found that ROS when measured in terms of PBDIT and PAT, it declined 12.45 per cent points to 25.33 per cent points respectively. This fall in PBDIT/sales ratio was statistically significant. ROE when measured in terms of PBDIT/equity, it declined by 11.77 per cent in terms of PBDIT/equity and 7.79 per cent when measured as PAT/equity were statistically significant. It was also found that the profitability in the disinvested enterprises declined because before 1991, these enterprises were doing business in protective environment but after 1991, New Industrial Policy (NIP) threw open new industries and services to private sector which were earlier completely reserved for public sector. Among these main PSEs were SAIL, ITI, HMT, Andrew Yule, BEML, HZL and HOCL.

Performance of disinvested PSEs under monopoly environment

Under the monopoly environment, 18 PSEs were selected for the purpose of this study. In order to examine the performance of disinvested PSEs, the profitability ratios were measured using Profit before depreciation, interest and tax (PBDIT) and Profit after tax (PAT) in the numerator of three sales ratios: Return on Sales (ROS), Return on Assets (ROA) and Return on Equity (ROE). It was found that profitability in terms of ROE declined after disinvestment while profitability in terms of ROS (PAT/sales) and ROA (PBDIT/assets) increased.

In some cases, petroleum companies like IOC, HPCL, BPRL, ONGC and GAIL and in telecommunication sector like VSNL and MTNL although there was increase in profits and turnover but in comparison to post 1991, equity, assets and sales increased more substantially resulted in negative mean after ratio for these PSEs. To conclude, profitability of disinvested enterprises increased marginally.

TABLE 6.4
Comparison of performance change in operating efficiency following disinvestment of PSEs operating in both competitive and monopoly environment

Parameter	*No. of PSEs*	*Mean before*	*Mean after*	*Change in mean (after - before)*	*t-value*
1. Sales efficiency (Return on sales/ No. of employees)					
Competitive	29	9.8214	8.1479	–1.6735	–1.1537
Monopoly	18	27.2186	29.8064	3.5878	2.0876

(Contd.)

2. Assets turnover (Sales/Total assets)					
Competitive	29	1.4261	1.4064	–0.0197	–0.4912
Monopoly	18	2.0837	1.8927	–0.1910	–0.6526
3. Employment (No. of employees)					
Competitive	29	25096	23167	–1929	–2.8912*
Monopoly	18	18873	20332	1459	0.9369
4. Dividend payout (Cash dividend/Net income)					
Competitive	29	0.1984	0.2602	0.0618	1.6452
Monopoly	18	0.1756	0.2389	0.0633	1.6894

*Found statistically significant.

Therefore, contrary to expectations sales efficiency, assets turnover ratio dropped instead of improving. Moreover competitive PSEs showed a marked decline vis-à-vis monopoly PSEs. While on the other hand, the expected relationship that there should be drop in employment level after disinvestment, increase in dividend payout is confirmed. But it was found that in case of monopoly enterprise, instead of decreasing, employment level increased exceptionally.

Profitability Change

In order to examine the impact of extent of disinvestment on financial performance, fourty-seven PSEs were divided into five groups as mentioned in Table 6.5, three profitability ratios ROS, ROA and ROE were examined separately. The findings reveal the followings:

1. Seventeen disinvested PSEs which were disinvested up to 10 per cent showed decline in terms of ROS and ROE which is statistically not significant individually. It was found that out of 17 disinvested enterprises National Fertilizers (NFL) and Nayveli Lignite Corp. (NLC) Ltd. showed increase in profitability ratios after disinvestment.
2. Five enterprises which were disinvested between 10 to 20 per cent, showed improvements in ROS, ROA and ROE (PAT/equity). The improvement in ROS (in terms of PAT/sales) was statistically significant. Remaining increase in profitability ratios was not statistically significant individually. Out of these five enterprises except IOC remaining four enterprises (MRL, SCI, SAIL and

Contd. on page 91

TABLE 6.5
Extent of disinvestment and changes in profitability

Parameter	*No. of PSEs*	*Mean before*	*Mean after*	*Change in mean (after - before)*	*t-value*
(A) Return on Sales					
1. Disinvestment up to 10%	17				
(a) PBDIT/Sales		0.3276	0.2875	–0.0401	–1.1327
(b) PAT/Sales		0.1492	0.1160	–0.0332	–1.0965
2. Disinvestment between 10–20%	5				
(a) PBDIT/Sales		0.2274	0.1466	–0.0808	–1.1998
(b) PAT/Sales		0.1132	0.2376	0.1244	–1.8547
3. Disinvestment between 20–30%	5				
(a) PBDIT/Sales		0.2968	0.2371	–0.0597	–1.1852
(b) PAT/Sales		0.0924	0.0689	–0.0235	–1.9978
4. Disinvestment between 30–40%	4				
(a) PBDIT/Sales		0.2883	0.2372	–0.0511	–2.5410
(b) PAT/Sales		0.1406	0.0981	–0.0425	–2.8435*
5. Disinvestment above 40%	16				
(a) PBDIT/Sales		0.2860	0.2964	–0.0204	0.7568
(b) PAT/Sales		0.0917	0.1836	0.0919	0.4562
(B) Return on Assets					
1. Disinvestment up to 10%	17				
(a) PBDIT/Assets		0.2346	0.2910	0.5640	0.9845
(b) PAT/Assets		0.0832	0.1492	0.0660	0.9657

(Contd.)

2. Disinvestment between 10–20%	5				
(a) PBDIT/Assets		0.2268	0.2506	0.0298	0.5413
(b) PAT/Assets		0.2212	0.2467	0.0745	0.6249
3. Disinvestment between 20–30%	5				
(a) PBDIT/Assets		0.2767	0.2312	–0.0455	–0.9847
(b) PAT/Assets		0.1246	0.0928	–0.0318	–1.8941
4. Disinvestment between 30–40%	4				
(a) PBDIT/Assets		0.2320	0.2846	0.5260	0.7258
(b) PAT/Assets		0.1261	0.1394	0.0133	0.2359
5. Disinvestment above 40%	16				
(a) PBDIT/Assets		0.2881	0.2779	–0.0102	–0.6851
(b) PAT/Assets		0.1276	0.1281	0.0005	0.1234
(C) Return on Equity					
1. Disinvestment up to 10%	17				
(a) PBDIT/Equity		0.3841	0.3461	–0.0380	–1.2543
(b) PAT/ Equity		0.1644	0.1436	–0.2080	–0.9857
2. Disinvestment between 10–20%	5				
(a) PBDIT/Equity		0.1609	0.1429	–0.0179	–1.9416
(b) PAT/Equity		0.4336	0.5280	0.0944	1.9874*
3. Disinvestment between 20–30%	5				
(a) PBDIT/Equity		0.6186	0.5377	–0.0849	–0.4657
(b) PAT/Equity		0.1418	0.1772	0.0354	1.8621
4. Disinvestment between 30–40%	4				
(a) PBDIT/Equity		0.4139	0.4382	0.0243	0.2640
(b) PAT/Equity		0.1383	0.1009	–0.0374	–0.6854
5. Disinvestment above 40%	16				
(a) PBDIT/Equity		0.5368	0.4862	–0.0506	–0.8756
(b) PAT/Equity		0.2006	0.1898	–0.0108	–0.6533

*Found statistically significant at 5% level.

NALCO) have shown improvements in profitability ratios after disinvestment. Drop in IOC was due to proportionate decrease in profitability vis-a-vis sales, equity and assets.

3. Five enterprises which were disinvested between 20 to 30 per cent, showed decline in terms of ROS, ROA, and ROE. This decline in ROA and ROE was statistically significant. Out of these five enterprises except ONGC remaining four enterprises (BRPL, ITI, Maruti and BEL) have shown decline in profitability ratios after disinvestment.
4. Four enterprises which were disinvested between 30 to 40 per cent, showed decline ROS and ROE. The drop in ROS (PAT/sales) is statistically significant whereas in other case it is not. Individually BEML, CONCOR have shown decrease in profitability in terms of ROS, ROA, ROE and BHEL has shown increase in profitability.
5. Sixteen enterprises which were disinvested above 40% have shown drop in ROA, ROE but marginal increase in ROS. However, none of them is statistically significant. At individual level, GAIL, CMC, ITDC and IPCL have shown increase in profitability while HOCL, HZL and VSNL have shown decline in profitability in terms of ROS, ROA and ROE.

To conclude, there is fall of profitability ratio when measured in terms of ROS, ROE and ROA unrelated to the degree of disinvestment. It was also found that enterprises those were performing well showed increase in overall profitability irrespective of the extent of disinvestment. (ONGC, IPCL, NFL, Neyali, SAIL, CMC, MRL, SCI, BHEL, NALCO and GAIL).

Changes in operational efficiency

In terms of sales efficiency

Sales efficiency when measured in terms of sub-samples of disinvested PSEs in terms of real sales/number of employees, it was found that enterprises which were disinvested up to thirty per cent showed decline in sales efficiency but it increased for those enterprises which were disinvested above thirty per cent but less than fourty per cent. This increase in sales efficiency was statistically significant for enterprises disinvested above thirty per cent. The others result were not statistically significant. At individual level in this group, CONCOR and BEML were exception where sales efficiency declined. In order to find out the reason, it was observed due to lack of orders from customers.

In terms of assets turnover

Assets turnover when measured under sub-samples of disinvested PSEs in terms of sales/total assets, it showed mixed findings. The enterprises which

Contd. on page 93

TABLE 6.6
Extent of disinvestment and operating efficiency

Parameter	*No. of PSEs*	*Mean before*	*Mean after*	*Change in mean (after - before)*	*t-value*
(A) Sales Efficiency (Return on sales/No. of employees)					
1. Disinvestment up to 10%	17	21.9862	21.8992	−0.0870	−0.8142
2. Disinvestment between 10–20%	5	24.0641	20.3264	−3.7377	−0.3464
3. Disinvestment between 20–30%	5	16.6820	14.8991	−1.7829	−0.3288
4. Disinvestment between 30–40%	4	8.4417	11.1832	2.7715	1.3461
5. Disinvestment above 40%	16	14.3983	14.8743	0.4760	1.8229*
(B) Assets Turnover (Sales/Total assets)					
1. Disinvestment up to 10%	17	1.9664	2.0864	0.1200	0.8214
2. Disinvestment between 10–20%	5	1.4831	1.2260	−0.2571	−1.8118
3. Disinvestment between 20–30%	5	1.3186	1.2864	−0.0322	−1.0236
4. Disinvestment between 30–40%	4	1.6439	1.9886	0.3447	1.4638
5. Disinvestment above 40%	16	2.1089	1.8324	−0.2765	−2.3880*
(C) Employment Level (Total employment)					
1. Disinvestment up to 10%	17	20877	19841	−1036	−2.0421
2. Disinvestment between 10–20%	5	23219	22089	−1129	−1.8764
3. Disinvestment between 20–30%	5	22841	21488	−1353	−1.7079
4. Disinvestment between 30–40%	4	19844	19734	−110	−1.8874
5. Disinvestment above 40%	16	21329	22804	1475	1.0429

*Found statistically significant at 5% level.

were disinvested above fourty per cent[1] showed decline in assets turnover ratio, which was statistically significant. In other cases, less or below than this category, findings were statistically not significant.

In terms of employment level

Employment level when measured in terms of number of total employees in case of sub samples of disinvested PSEs, it showed that level of employees for enterprises disinvested up to fourty per cent declined continuously. On the other hand, it increased for enterprises disinvested above fourty per cent. However, none of these was statistically significant.

TABLE 6.7
Summary of results for financial efficiency in the full sample of 47 disinvested PSEs

Profitability	*Mean before*	*Mean after*	*Changes in mean (after - before)*	*'t' value*
Return on Sales (ROS)				
(a) PBDIT/Sales	0.3651	0.2708	–0.0943	–3.135*
(b) PAT/Sales	0.1383	0.0213	–0.1170	–1.998
Return on Equity (ROE)				
(a) PBDIT/Equity	0.5769	0.4632	–0.1137	–2.5648*
(b) PAT/Equity	0.1733	0.1066	–0.0667	–2.0043*
Return on Assets (ROA)				
(a) PBDIT/Total assets	0.3664	0.3417	–0.0247	–0.9432
(b) PAT/Total assets	0.0987	0.0843	–0.0144	–0.6886

* Statistically significant.

After the analysis of Table 6.7, following observations were made for the full sample of disinvested public enterprises:

(i) There was a drop in ROS after disinvestment (by 9.43%) when measured by PBDIT/sales and on the other hand, it showed 11.7% drop when calculated on the basis of PAT/sales. This downfall is statistically significant.

(ii) In terms of ROA, it also showed decline both in terms of PBDIT/assets and PAT/assets, which is statistically not significant.

(iii) When profitability was measured in terms of ROE, it declined both in terms of PBDIT/equity and PAT/equity (by 11.37% when measured by PBDIT/equity and 6.67% when measured by PAT/equity).

Other observations are:

(a) It was also observed that some disinvested public enterprises showed decline in profitability because before their disinvestment, they were doing business in a fully or partly protected environment. But with the start of new economic policy, they have been facing cut-throat competition from their private counterparts under no umbrella of protection. For instance, after disinvestment, the monopolistic position of MMTC, BEML and STC went down and consequently profitability and their sales were reduced and still the condition seems to remain same in the years to come.

(b) On the other hand, some enterprises which are still in monopolistic environment are making profits or showing growth year after year, to name a few, are: GAIL, ONGC, HPCL and BPCL.

Impact of New Economic Policy on Indian Corporate Sector

The new economic policy takes some solid steps regarding the corporate restructuring, like (i) portfolio of PSEs, investments would be focused on strategic, high-tech and essential infrastructure, (ii) sick PSEs should be referred to Board of Industrial and Financial Reconstruction (BIFR) etc. This new economic policy remained effective, as profitability increased in the initial years till 1995-96, since then no positive sign of improvement has been seen so far. Table 6.8 brings out that in case of manufacturing sector, public sector has not shown any remarkable improvement as compared to their private counterparts. Here the percentage changes under seven different heads, such as, sales, gross fixed assets, debt/equity etc. have been shown.

TABLE 6.8
Profitability ratios in corporate sector (Manufacturing companies)

	Units	*1999-00*	*2000-01*	*2001-02*	*2002-03*	*2003-04*
Sales	% change	16.9	17.1	–0.3	11.2	11.7
Public Sector	% change	29.5	23.2	–4.9	14.9	10.3
Private Sector	% change	11.5	14.2	2.1	9.3	12.5
Gross Fixed Assets	% change	12.3	10.4	9.6	6.3	5.6
Public Sector	% change	11.1	11.1	5.7	5.5	5.0
Private Sector	% change	12.8	10.2	10.8	6.6	5.7
PBDIT	% change	8.3	7.6	1.5	23.0	19.1
Public Sector	% change	–0.6	7.8	6.5	62.1	23.6
Private Sector	% change	10.5	7.6	0.5	14.1	17.7

(Contd.)

Profit after tax	% change	–7.1	–3.0	–	3460.8	84.6
Public Sector	% change	–	–	–	–	111.3
Private Sector	% change	11.2	–10.7	–48.5	178.1	75.0
PBDIT/Sales	per cent	10.4	9.6	9.7	10.7	11.6
Public Sector	per cent	5.8	5.2	5.5	7.9	8.9
Private Sector	per cent	12.7	11.9	11.6	12.2	13.0
PAT/Sales	per cent	0.5	0.5	–0.1	1.7	3.4
Public Sector	per cent	–1.1	–0.6	–1.5	1.2	3.1
Private Sector	per cent	1.3	1.1	0.6	2.0	3.6
Debt/Equity	times	1.51	1.55	1.67	1.58	1.26
Public Sector	times	2.96	3.36	6.41	4.68	1.83
Private Sector	times	1.32	1.33	1.36	1.33	1.17

Source: www.cmie.com

Impact on Operational Performance

To examine the impact of disinvestment on operational performance, three parameters, *viz.* sales efficiency, employment and assets turnover were taken for these disinvested public enterprises. The results of these parameters are shown in Table 6.9. It shows the changes in operational performance for the complete sample of disinvested PSEs, when changes in mean between mean after and mean before were taken.

TABLE 6.9
Summary of results for operational efficiency in the full sample of 47 disinvested PSEs

Parameter	*Mean before*	*Mean after*	*Changes in mean (after - before)*	*'t' value*
Sales Efficiency (Real sales/No. of employees)	19.4482	21.7136	2.2654	0.4297
Employment (Total employees)	23916	22407	–1509	–2.315
Assets Turnover (Sales/Total assets)	1.5729	1.4595	–0.1134	–0.6732
Dividend Payout (Cash dividend/Net income)	0.1973	0.2744	0.0771	1.9133*
Leverage (Debt to assets)	0.5342	0.4348	–0.0994	–2.9874*

* Statistically significant.

After analysis of Table 6.9, following observations were made for the full sample of disinvested PSEs.

Changes in sales efficiency

When sales efficiency was measured in terms of real sales per employee, it showed positive change after the disinvestment from a figure of Rs. 19.44 lakh to Rs. 21.71 lakh. Out of these disinvested PSEs, some enterprises like MRL, GAIL, ONGC, HPCL and BPCL showed major improvement while some enterprises like BEML, ITI, STC and MMTC showed major downfall due to loss of their monopolistic situation in the country.

Changes in employment

In this regard, it is very difficult to explain the exact picture whether there was any downfall in employment because many disinvested PSEs have offered voluntary retirement scheme (VRS) and still some enterprises have been offering VRS to offload employees' burden. The analysis of sample shows that overall employment in disinvested PSEs reduced by an average of 1509 employees. This figure is not statistically significant.

Changes in assets turnover

The average assets turnover, which was measured in terms of sales/total assets, declined for these disinvested PSEs by 11.34 per cent. Contrary to the expectation, assets turnover declined instead of improving. However, this figure is not statistically significant.

Changes in leverage

Leverage ratio, measured in terms of (total debts/total assets) dropped as was expected and was statistically significant.

Changes in dividend payout

Dividend payout ratio (calculated in terms of cash/dividend) for the full sample of forty-seven disinvested PSEs increased from 19.73 to 27.44 per cent after disinvestment. Total increase in dividend payout ratio was 7.63 per cent, which is statistically significant. One point in this regard should be noted that during FY 1995 and 1996, Ministry of Finance had issued some guidelines regarding minimum dividend to be distributed in some public sectors, like petroleum, chemical and oil sector dividend cannot be less than 29 per cent of post-tax profit. Therefore, what was the exact cause behind increase in the dividend payout is not clear, but there should be no doubt in saying that the change in the government policy has big impact on increase in the dividend payout.

Conclusion

Under the ongoing drive of disinvestment, the government has mainly targeted most of the blue chip, profit-making PSEs, which were decorated with the classification of 'Ratnas'. The strategy behind this drive seems to erase the public sector network from the industrial map of India. The analysis of these disinvested PSEs describes that after the disinvestment drive, the financial performance, which was measured in terms of ROS, ROA and ROE decreased.

The examination of operational performance of these disinvested PSEs states that sales efficiency improved after disinvestment, when measured in terms of real sales/number of employees.

On the other hand, the level of employment reduced as was expected initially after disinvestment. One cause behind this decline may be due to the introduction of VRS in the disinvested PSEs, as after the launch of New Industrial Policy (1991), pressure increased on PSEs and number of companies resorted to VRS.

Leverage ratio, measured in terms of (total debts/total assets) dropped as was expected and was statistically significant for these disinvested PSEs. Also assets turnover ratio when measured in terms of sales/total assets declined. In the light of the analysis of these disinvested PSEs it appears that envisaged goal of disinvestment is not fully achieved. While examining the reasons, it was found that the majority of the enterprises which showed drop in profitability were those which previously operating in competitive sector but were protected or favoured to some extent. But post 1991, they were no longer favoured. For example, after 1991, with the deregulation of steel industry, SAIL's profitability declined from 1996-97 and even it continued losses from 1999-2000 onwards. Further, due to rationalization of sale price in line with global prices, profitability of Hindustan Zinc and Hindustan Copper Ltd., declined significantly, also with decanalisation of trade, almost monopoly position of MMTC and STC in international trade was almost eliminated resulting in deterioration of profitability. Most of the PSEs faced lack of orders due to severe competition from existing customers. For example, BEML (from defence and Indian railways), ITI (from DOT[2]) resulting in overall reduced profitability. However, the fertilizer sector (RCFL, NFL, and FACT) continued under pricing mechanism[3] which assured positive post tax return on net worth. In nutshell with budgetary support reduced and preferential access to bank credit eliminated, many PSEs recorded a dip in earnings. The expected result was that after disinvestment profitability should go up, rejecting null hypothesis. On the contrary, the profitability declined.

While examining whether the extent of disinvestment makes any difference in performance of enterprises, it was found that for partly disinvested enterprises where control still lies in government hands, the results of degree of disinvestment on profitability, sales efficiency, employment, assets turnover showed mixed findings. Therefore, it appears that at individual level these parameters did not depend on extent of disinvestment but rather depended on the particular enterprise. In short, there is a lowering of profitability in terms of ROS, ROA and ROE, and that is also have no relation with the extent of disinvestment. Though as was expected, dividend payout ratio increased in the disinvested enterprises when sub-samples examined. It seems that the performance level instead of depending upon the extent of disinvestment is actually dependent on the managerial policies, philosophy and procedures of a particular enterprise. One point in this regard should not be left undiscussed that the performance level sometimes may not change due to change in the government policies and economic environment but rather due to disinvestment drive. It was also observed that competition and monopolistic situation of an enterprise are also the key determinant of success, of a public sector enterprise.

Therefore, opposite to expectations, profitability, assets turnover, instead of improving, declined. The expected relationship that there would be drop in employment levels, and improvement in sales efficiency is confirmed. However, changes in enterprise performance could be due to changes in the competitive environment and not because of disinvestment. This is predominantly correct where disinvestment is part of a broader process of economic liberalization and deregulation.

NOTES

1. BALCO, GAIL, CMC, HOCL, HPCL, HTL, HZL, IBP, IPCL, MTNL, MFIL, PPL, VSNL, Jessop & Ltd., ITDC, STC.
2. Department of Telecommunications.
3. Generally the price mechanism is the method through which the market organizes and adjusts itself. Prices determine what is produced, how it's produced and who receives the product. If the market is working correctly, the workings of the price mechanism should result in the most efficient allocation of resources.

REFERENCES

1. CHADHA, S.K. *Disinvestment of Selected Public Enterprises,* in the Indian Journal of Public Administration, Vol. XLVII, No. 2, April-June 2001.
2. DAS, P.M. *FI's Draws Up Priority List for Disinvestment in IBP, MMTC, STC,* in The Economic times, November 10, 1999.
3. ECONOMY BUREAU. *Govt. Seeks Private Role in Coal Sector,* in Business Standard, New Delhi, November 1, 2000.
4. RAMAKRISHNA, G.V. (1996). *Report on Disinvestment,* Ministry of Finance, Government of India.
5. RAMANA, G.V. *PSU Disinvestment; Why The Tearing Hurry?,* Economic Times, January 21, 1992.
6. RANGARAJAN, C. (2000). *Indian Economy—Essays on Money and Finance,* UBS Publishers, New Delhi, pp. 287-293.
7. SEN, A. AND GUPTA. *Disinvesting in the Oil Companies,* the Economic Times, September 12, 2000.
8. SHAM. *Disinvestments,* The Economic Times, September 6, 2000.

CHAPTER 7

SUMMARY AND CONCLUSIONS

Effect of New Economic Policy (1991) on Disinvested PSEs

The New Industrial Policy announced in July 1991, besides liberalisation of economy and globalisation, was aimed at building upon the gains achieved, to correct the distortions, maintain a sustained growth in productivity, gainful employment and in attaining international competitiveness. All sectors of industry whether small, medium or large, belonging to public, private or cooperative sectors were to be encouraged to grow and improve on their post performance. It was found that post 1991, the performance of PSEs in terms of profitability ratios and operational efficiency, instead of improving has declined despite of disinvestment and consecutive public sector specific reforms. This decline may be due to environmental factors such as competition, cheaper products, continuing with the old technology, lack of training or firm specific factors like old management styles, attitudes of workers and employees towards management policies etc. To examine these aspects, and in-depth analysis of PSEs from diverse fields like petroleum (HPCL), steel (SAIL), engineering (BEL), fertilizers (PPL, NFL) was done during measurement of financial and operational performance of disinvested PSEs. The prime motive behind studying such individual enterprises was to know the impact of changed environment on PSEs. These are the following observations:

(a) The main constraint in the functioning of PSEs today is concerning them as 'public sector enterprises' in the constitution. Consequently, it provides supplementary protection to PSEs' employees and workers and subject to multiple bureaucratic controls. Such interference is a great problem faced during the disinvestment process. It is not only the politicians who interfere but also the multiple masters, to name a few—the minister, the secretary in charge of the ministry, bureau of public enterprises, planning commission, the finance ministry play a vital role in decision-taking process and its implementation. For instance, despite overcrowding of employees in most of the PSEs, government for their selfish motives raised the retirement age from 58 to 60 years.

(b) It was observed that profitability of many PSEs declined mainly due to environmental factors such as continuing with traditional methods to produce more or less modern products, locational disadvantage, recession and reducing entry barriers in Indian industry after fiscal 1996-97. (SAIL, VSNL, BEML, GAIL, ITDC, ITI, ICI and MUL). However, SAIL was subject to several firm specific factors like overmanning, cut-throat competition, uncontrollable costs and soaring interest burden, due to which SAIL's profitability suffered.

(c) PSEs, which had sound Corporate Planning Group, R & D cell and Institutionalized Mechanism for monitoring and diagnosing the environmental factors like development in technology, could respond better and in effective manner to the environmental changes. (VSNL, BHEL, IOC, GAIL and SAIL)

(d) The New Industrial Policy (NIP) brought far-reaching changes in the industrial sector. Customers have profited in terms of quality, high technology products, wider range of products in comparatively affordable prices. Such as switching and transmission equipments, steel, earth moving, and telephone equipments.

(e) Resource wealthy PSEs were able to diversify its activities to take advantage of new emerging opportunities. (IOC and VSNL). IOC has entered into various joint ventures to acquire new technologies. For example, with Avi Oil India for defence aviation lubricants, Indo Mobil for premium lubricants, Indian Oil Tanking Ltd. for tankage infrastructure and Petronet India Ltd. for pipelines[1].

(f) Monopolistic PSEs which have not faced competition hitherto (IOC, BEL, NLC, BRPL and NFL) have not successful in their cost reduction measures.

(g) Post 1991, most of the PSEs are investing considerable sum in training to make all employees more cost conscious. Like IOC through training, it is making all employees understand the implication of deregulation in terms of future opportunities and threats. It was observed that chiefly in high technology based areas (MTNL, VSNL, IOC, IBP and NTPC) responsible employees have been joining private sector for good offerings. Therefore, the real advantage of training and development has gone to private sector instead of public sector.

Impact of competition

Prior to New Industrial Policy of 1991, due to monopoly of public sector, there was not much competition. PSEs like NFL, ITI, VSNL, HMT, BALCO, MTNL, BEL and IOC, which prior to 1991 were in monopoly, faced severe competition and their production cost due to ignorance of cost-cutting factor increased sharply. Like, competition forced ITI to adopt marginal costing which has resulted in very less margins. The pressures on margin can be deducted from the fact that in ITI during FY 2000 the value of production despite being 2100 crore, profit was only around 27 crore. It seems that the decline in profitability is more on account of environmental factors such as increased competition and deregulation and not because of disinvestment factor only.

On the other hand, customers enjoyed cheaper advanced products (MUL, HMT) and services (VSNL, MTNL) at lower prices with far better quality.

Impact on policy matters

Increased competition forced the public sector to enter into new areas in order to retain their market share and profitability by way of diversifying the product line. Now PSEs instead of investing in traditional sectors like MTNL and VSNL, started business operations in mobile industry and as an Internet service provider, totally new areas for them.

To build a new image amongst consumers, all the PSEs became market-oriented and started providing new products and new models to customers to remain in the market.

PSEs like SAIL, BALCO, HMT, H Cab Ltd. and PPL having limited resources became more focused in their activities in order to sustain their identity.

PSEs like BEML, BHEL, ONGC, IIT and BEL tried to now focus on such areas where profits are comparatively more and competition was less such as supplies to defence.

PSEs have been contributing greatly to the export earnings of our country. Earnings have been steadily increasing and they peaked during 1995-96, with record earnings of Rs. 17,831.5 crore. Manufacturing and services have contributed to this peak performance. (HZL, PPL, HOCL, BEML, BEL, ONGC, CONCOR, Neyeli Lignite and SCI).

Effect of Disinvestment on Performance of PSEs

Disinvestment, which has become a universal trend, implies transfer of ownership and/or management of an enterprise from the public sector to a private sector. It began in India in 1991-92 with the sale of minority stakes in some PSEs. Disinvestment today is a very important aspect of the economic reforms in India. Over the last two decades, the disinvestment has become a vital measure of economic rejuvenation. Even in the 'communist' countries, it has become a universal trend. In India, forty-eight enterprises have been disinvested to varying extent till mid 2004. Despite selling the equity in private hands, the government continued to retain control over them by selling the equity below 49 per cent mark.

In order to examine whether anticipated goal of improvement in the performance of disinvested PSEs was attained or not, profitability in terms of Return on Equity (ROE), Return on Assets (ROA) and Return on Sales (ROS) was analyzed. In order to examine the operational efficiency assets turnover, sales efficiency, dividend payout ratio and employment factors were analyzed. It was observed that after the disinvestment, overall performance of disinvested PSEs deteriorated in terms of profitability and operating ratios instead of improvement.

Effect of Extent of Disinvestment on Performance of PSEs

In order to examine the impact of extent of disinvestment, the enterprises were divided into five groups from less than 10 per cent to greater than 40 per cent disinvestment. In this regard, it seems contrary to our presumption that disinvestment results in improved profitability, as performance declined after disinvestment. In case of partly disinvested PSEs, where still the control is in the government hands, it showed mixed results.

It has also been confirmed that disinvestment results in increase in dividend payout ratio, decline in employment ratio and improvement in sales efficiency. At first glance, it seemed contradictory, so efforts were made to find out the reasons behind this decline in performance that took place in post 1991 period.

On the basis of in-depth examination of enterprises from diverse fields like petroleum, fertilizer, steel and engineering sectors, following reasons were found out:

(i) Liberalization policy of Government of India opened the doors for foreign trades those were offering cheaper products and services, caused a sharp decline in the sales of these PSEs, like SAIL, BEML and BHEL etc.

(ii) Abolition of licensing policy for all industries, except those related to strategic and security concerns, environmental and social reasons related irrespective of the levels of investment, invited small-scale industries and foreign companies to sell their products vis-à-vis PSEs. This exemption from licensing was particularly helpful to many dynamic small and medium entrepreneurs who have been unnecessarily hampered by the licensing system. Therefore, PSEs like BEML and SAIL due to unawareness could not run in this new economic era and suffered losses.

(iii) World Trade Organization (WTO) treaty did not give enough time to those PSEs that were used to run on government subsidies under retention price mechanism. National Fertilizer Limited (NFL) is the best example that suffered a lot because of deregulation of fertilizer sector.

Secondly, one thing should be noted here that all PSEs have self-identities and it is an apex body of Government of India. There are chairmen-cum-managing directors, who are looking day-to-day operations of these PSEs and are responsible for all acts. It was found that there was no change in the management after the disinvestment as a result there has been as such no qualitative change in the monitoring mechanism, work culture, decision-making styles of disinvested enterprise.

To conclude, the hypothesis that degree of disinvestment will lead to improved efficiency and profitability does not hold validate. Hence, it is not the degree but the managerial competitiveness and other market factors such as innovation, state of technology, government interference which affect the profitability in real sense.

Effect of Ownership on Efficiency

It is generally believed that in public sector enterprises neither incentives nor sanctions are closely related to efficiency. Also, the 'private right theory' suggests that PSEs show fewer profits and are less efficient than their private counterparts. Several studies have been conducted both in India as well as abroad, with mixed findings about their relative efficiency. Despite these mixed findings, efforts were made in this research study to draw conclusions regarding the relative efficiency of both public and private sectors. The conclusions are summed up as follows:

1. It was observed that performance chiefly depends upon the nature of competition, which is the driving force. Therefore, when markets are deregulated, the performance of firms, whether public or private, improves. There are several reasons why competitive forces result in improved performance.
   (a) Competition provides opportunity to manufacturers, to launch a new product or to modify their existing products from time to time in order to sustain their market share before competitors come with new technology. (VSNL, MTNL, ITI, BEL, MUL and BEML)
   (b) Entry of newcomers in the same business threats the existing market players to work in a systematic manner with hard work and implementation of new ideas, resulting in improved performance. (BPCL, IOC, ONGC, GAIL, MRL, HPCL, CONCOR, BHEL, VSNL and Neyali Lignite Corporation Ltd.)
2. When market power is significant as in the case of regulated or natural monopolies such as petroleum (IOC, BRPL, LRL, MRL and BPCL), power (NTPC) and electricity sector (NHPC), there is no efficiency difference between public and private firms. Hence, there is little empirical justification in favour of either type of ownership.
3. It was also observed side by side that managerial capability, efficiency of managers, education level and job security factor are closely related to performance. Unlike public sector, private sector employees have no such job security therefore, in order to get advancement and to secure their job, employees work more and harder resulting in improved performance. This is one of the main reasons why trained and experienced employees in high technology sector were offered and hired by private sector. (VSNL, MTNL, GAIL, HPCL and IOC) for instance, nearly fourty per cent of the work force in Reliance Group (pertaining to oil and telecom) is hired from public sector.[2]

Observations and Recommendations

Budgetary burden and public

The disinvestment process began in India in 1991-92 with the sale of minority stakes in some PSEs. From 1999-2000 onwards, the focus shifted to strategic sales. Despite this, the accumulated losses of many PSEs are larger than the capital invested in them. These public sector deficits compel the government to increase taxation and curtail development expenditures. There is no justification for imposing such burden on the public by the state carrying out activities, which the private sector can do more efficiently. Therefore, disinvestment of certain sectors likes hotel industry, soap, buses, detergents, cosmetics, bread and variety of other eatables, which can be better performed by the private sector, is necessary to reduce the budgetary burden on the public and to relieve the consumers from the indifferent and arrogant attitude of the public sector.

What should be the role of government in PSEs?

We are reminded of what John Maynard Keynes once said, "The important thing for Government is not to do things that individuals are doing already, and to do them a little better or a little worse; but to do those things which at present are not done at all". What is not done till now is the improvement of social sector: primary education, health, housing, infrastructure, nutrition and the like. Let the Government concentrate on these areas.

The findings of this research study also suggest that the Government should withdraw from areas where private sector can do better. Like food (MFIL), steel (SAIL), chemical and pharmaceuticals (IPCL, HIL and HOCL). Today, India has achieved a certain level of industrial development and private entrepreneurship is in plenty (Tourist Services, Telecom Services), therefore, the state should curtail its entrepreneurial role and concentrate on its resources on the promotional and regulatory role.[3]

Ownership and performance

There is no doubt in saying that disinvestment of PSEs enables the government to mop up funds. It was found that it is the people who matter the most and not the ownership. If the enterprises are sick, it is because of the people who manage them are sick. Unfortunately, it is observed that such people manage all the loss-making PSEs. These few elites have considered PSEs to be their properties meant for private use. Recent disinvestment of some enterprises like disinvestment of hotels of ITDC group suggested that ownership can bring a drastic change in performance. This episode was capable enough to open the eyes of makers of disinvestment policy that how mismanagement has eaten up the vitals of ITDC group. Therefore, it is recommended that salary structures and bonuses of the top management should be linked to performance parameters of a PSE. Performance assessment should be carried out at routine intervals.

Employees' welfare

In order to protect workers' interests, employees of the disinvested units are to be allowed to buy shares. A scheme of preferential offer of shares to workers and employees should be devised. Like, in 2004-05 for the first time, five per cent shares of IPCL were offered to its employees.

Introduction of claw back mechanism

To make the disinvestment process transparent, claw back mechanism (which involves allocation of a certain percentage of shares to small investors), and instalment purchases of shares should be introduced to general public at a fixed price through a general prospecting.

Liberalization and its aftermath

On 24th July, 1991 the government headed by Mr. P.V. Narsimha Rao, announced a new industrial policy, which sought to drastically alter the industrial scenario in our country. It gave birth to new era decorated with liberalization and globalization. It resulted in overall improved efficiency due to competitive threats upon the managers. The competition is in favour of customers as they get new variety, advanced technology, good quality at right price, right time and at right place. Today, customers need not go to market for buying goods but home delivery has become the fashion of the day. In order to improve the performance of public sector, management of PSEs has become market-oriented in terms of variety of products and quality by concentrating on R & D cell. (SAIL, IOC, MUL, BHEL, ITI, BEL and BEML) for instance, the management of BEML claims that R & D is strength of BEML and its average turnover of ten per cent is on account of new products.

Similarly, there is a strong emphasis on training in most of the PSEs like IOC, has 17 training centres and an apex institute—Indian Oil Institute of Petroleum Management.

Importance of price mechanism

It is strongly recommended that disinvestment will do more harm than any good if selling of monopolistic PSEs take place without either breaking them up or creating mechanisms to regulate their prices. (BALCO, NFL, PPL, SAIL and MFIL)

Sound method of valuation

There have been several criticisms of the disinvestment process. An important and perhaps most critical issue in the process of disinvestment of PSEs is the valuation. Be it disinvestment of 1991-92 or that of BALCO in 2001, valuation has always been at the core of controversy. This is so because there are several methods of valuation and different methods yield widely varying results. The critically of the issue of valuation in disinvestment can be easily gauged from the fact that value of BALCO as put by different people differed as widely as from Rs. 1,100 crore to Rs. 5,000 crore. Therefore, it is recommended for the well-being of nation, sound method of valuation should be evolved. Nonetheless, what is important is that not merely should the value derived be unquestionable on the basis of well established equity valuation principles, but also the processes and methodologies adopted for deriving such value be reasonable. To avoid controversies, transparency in valuations is must.

Tenure of the CEOs and board of directors

Generally, the managerial problems in the PSEs begin with the tenure of CEOs and Board of Directors. In India, the selection, service conditions and the tenure of the Board of Directors is subject to the Government rules and regulations. Unlike the private sector where CEO has almost a decade to nurture the company, in PSEs the rules with respect to superannuating tends to focus attention on short-term strategies co-terminus with CEO's tenure. Hence, there is a need to provide continuity in the management by appointing CEO and other members in the Board of Directors for longer tenure with representation of shareholders.

Change in ownership

Disinvestment must not result in greater concentration of assets. Rather it should ensure greater competition through more dispersed ownership. Though the process of disinvestment was set in motion sometime back, still no concrete efforts have been made to disperse sales widely. What has happened till now is that the divested equity between five and twenty per cent of most of the PSEs has merely changed hands within the government, *i.e.*, from the government to mutual funds and financial institutions, which are again owned by the government. For instance, in 2005-06 only, the government collected Rs. 1567.60 crore by sale of shares to public sector financial institutions and public sector banks on 'different pricing method'. Only a handful of scrips are listed and trading volumes in them are thin. Therefore, best method for disinvestment is 'public issue', which involves sale of shares to the public at large. Like Maruti had launched (27.5%) its IPO in 2003-04 which got tremendous response from public.

Sound policy framework

In 2001-02 Government decided to sell six hotels owned by the Indian Tourism Development Corporation (ITDC) while the two Five Star Ashoka Hotels in Delhi and Bangalore on 30 years lease to the private parties. In addition the three Centaur Hotels run by the Hotel Corporation of India in Delhi and Mumbai were selected to hive off along with the Chefair subsidiary and small Hotel Rajgir. The transaction documents for the sale was cleared by the Cabinet Committee on Disinvestment (CCD) setting the stage for disinvesting Government equity in these 13 entities for which the price bids will be invited.

For disinvestment of hotels, the Government of India invited bid from the public. 124 bidders submitted for purchase of these properties of which 97 had shown interest in the ITDC hotels and 18 in the HCL hotels. But ultimately, government decided to stagger the bidding since it was difficult for so many bidders to arrange for bank guarantees altogether. Therefore, it is suggested to government without doing proper ground work no such major decision should be taken.

Winding up

Political interference has become the common problem faced by the public sector units. Be it location of the enterprises, appointment of chief executives or any other factor, interference by political leaders is coming in the way of effective functioning of PSEs. As it is well known, many PSEs were set-up in backward areas for political reasons. But inadequate infrastructure, which had to be built up, haulage of raw materials from long distances and transport of, finished goods to far away markets hiked up both project and operational costs (NFL, BALCO). Often the labour available in the backward areas was not well trained to handle technology of the enterprise, with the result, sub-standard products were dished out, which were promptly rejected by buyers. It is suggested that chronically loss-making such units should be allowed to die a natural death. Bharat Gold Mines and Scooters Limited is an example of such kind. Therefore, it is recommended that these PSEs should be wound up at the earliest.

Multiple audit

The business decision in PSEs gets influenced by the presence of number of controlling agencies, such as the Ministry, Parliamentary Committees, CVC,

CAG, etc. subsequently resulting in recoursing to a risk adverse approach to business. Therefore, in this era of cut-throat global competition, there should be decisions, which bring substantial gain to the company. In this regard, the role of ministry also needs to change. Like a shareholder of any other company, the ministry's role should be limited to contributing as shareholder in the annual general meetings etc. of the companies. Also the role of ministry in day-to-day management through correspondence should be avoided.

Decentralization of powers

The Board of Directors of a public sector enterprise should be empowered to hive off a portion of its assets, either as a joint venture entity or as an independent subsidiary without being subjected to vetting by a government's decision-making process.

Powers to form joint ventures

PSEs should be allowed to form joint ventures with Indian or foreign companies in which the partner holds less than or equal stakes. Under article 12 of the Constitution, the public sector is subject to too many scrutinies and is answerable to many committees. These committees instead of raising efficiency have become courts where most of the PSEs managements' valuable time are lost in answering the questions. Therefore, PSEs should be taken out of the purview of article 12 of the Constitution.

Objectives of disinvestment

Disinvestment, as is pointed earlier is a global phenomenon. It is interesting to note that in India the real objective of disinvestment is another problem. Is it for raising revenue? Is it for making the enterprise competitive? If there are multiple objectives, what is the priority list? It is, therefore, strongly recommended that the objective of disinvestment whatever is, should be to improve the performance of PSEs so as to lessen the financial burden on taxpayers. The other objective should aim at increasing the size and dynamism of the private sector, distributing ownership more widely in the population at large, encouraging and facilitating private sector investments from both domestic and foreign sources, generating the revenues for the state and reducing the inventory burden on the state.

Reasons for Slow Achievements

Why Indian government did not achieve the target year after year? The following reasons were identified:

1. As expected, the amount realized through disinvestment proceed was not paid to the enterprise concerned for its expansion and improving efficiency but the Government has been using such disinvestment proceeds to bridge the budget deficit and in non-plan expenditures.
2. Absence of sound valuation process, procedures and surplus employees are other major attributes. It was estimated that in almost each enterprise, 15–25% employees were in excess.
3. The Government is not transparent about its approach towards sequencing the corporate restructuring and methods of disinvestment of PSEs.
4. The offers made by the Government for disinvestment of PSEs are not striking and painstaking bureaucratic procedures discourage the private sector interest to participate in disinvestment bids.
5. One reason can be cited for this failure is the non-acceptability of the shares of PSEs in the capital market.
6. The unfavourable market conditions like lengthy paper work, red tapism, political pressure from alliance parties are the main responsible for this downward trend of disinvestment.

General Suggestions

1. Before offering shares to private parties, a scheme of preferential offer of shares to workers and employees should be devised. It will be more relevant and beneficial to offer their equities to employees of the PSE concerned as it was done by Margaret Thatcher, the Prime Minister of U.K. and was welcome by all and sundry.
2. Disinvestment process should be transparent.
3. In areas of strategic importance like defence and atomic energy, the government should retain majority holdings in the equity of these PSEs.
4. To get the best possible price from bidders, disinvestment process should be in stages and sales must be staggered.
5. It will be beneficial for both the government and general public if disinvested shares are offered to public at a fixed price through a general prospectus.
6. The way the disinvestment process is pushed through clearly reveals that no adequate homework was done before the process was set in motion. Due to this, the government did not achieve the targeted amount year after year. Therefore, proper policy and route

regarding units to be disinvested should be clearly identified in advance considering all pros and cons.

7. To monitor the process of disinvestment a parallel body should be set-up.
8. Political interference is a great problem faced during the disinvestment process. It is not only the politicians who interfere but also the multiple masters, to name a few—the minister, the secretary incharge of the ministry, bureau of public enterprises, planning commission, the finance ministry play a vital role in decision-taking process and its implementation. However, disinvestment to be successful requires political boldness and the government should show the required political boldness in the matter of disinvestment.
9. All loss-making public sector enterprises should be privatized or closed or sold, which cannot be revived.
10. The extent of disinvestment in PSEs should be spread to each sector of economy.
11. Disinvestment proceeds should go to a fund dedicated to social sectors schemes.
12. Instead of year-wise targets of disinvestment, long-term disinvestment programme should be evolved.
13. In all non-strategic profitable companies, disinvestments should be up to 74 per cent and in all strategic profitable enterprises disinvestments should be up to 49 per cent.
14. All PSEs have self-identities and it is an apex body of government of India. There are chairmen-cum-managing directors, who are looking day-to-day problem and they are responsible for all acts. It is suggested to the central government that under the economic liberalization policy, the government should work on the theory of revenue v/s payment of salary of employee. It means that earning of individual PSE should distribute among their employees' salary in the proportionate ratio from top to bottom. If they are not able to earn equivalent to their salaries, then their salaries should held up or cut in proportionate ratio. The central government should not be responsible for the misdeed of employees and liable to pay their salaries from public money. In this way the central government should fix responsibility on each and every employee of an organization, *i.e.*, PSEs. It is also suggested that central government should give more liberty of their PSEs to act free and fare for national interest and profit making.
15. The central government should not act on the suggestion of American Government that all PSEs should be disinvested for

private sector and foreign buyers. It may be a conspiracy against our nation, as foreign investors do not want to invest huge capital in any industry in India. They want to earn more in respect of their investment. It is only the safe passes that they will get total infrastructure without investing any time and getting more and more benefits through profit-making PSEs. It is only the way that they want to invest less capital and earn more money on the national cost.

Current Status of Ministry of Disinvestment

After the defeat of National Democratic Alliance (NDA) in 14th Lok Sabha elections, the new coalition government, with left parties supporting the Congress came into power, has wound up the Ministry of Disinvestment. Because the leftist group which is supporting the UPA government, is opposed to disinvestment, as such, on the ideological ground. The Common Minimum Programme (CMP) of the United Progressive Alliance (UPA) follows privatization of loss-making firms on a transparent and consultative case-by-case basis. The UPA will retain existing 'navratna' companies in the public sector while these companies raise resources from the capital market. While every effort will be made to modernize and restructure sick public sector companies and revive sick industry, chronically loss-making companies will either be sold-off, or closed, after all workers have got their legitimate dues and compensation. The UPA will induct private industry to turn around companies that have potential for revival.

The UPA Government believes that disinvestment should increase competition, not decrease it. It will not support the emergence of any monopoly that only restricts competition. It also believes that there must be a direct link between disinvestment and social needs like, for example, the use of privatization revenues for designated social sector schemes. Public sector companies and nationalized banks will be encouraged to enter the capital market to raise resources and offer new investment avenues to retail investors.

Calling off of the ongoing cases of strategic sale

In conformity with the policy enunciated in CMP, it was decided in February 2005 to formally call off the process of *disinvestment through strategic sale* of profit making PSEs, as enumerated below:

List of strategic sale cases called off

Sl. No.	*Name of the PSEs*	*Percentage of equity which was earlier proposed to be sold through strategic sale*
1.	Manganese Ore India Limited	51%
2.	Sponge Iron India Limited	100%
3.	Shipping Corporation of India Limited	54.12% (51% through strategic sale and 3.12% to employees)
4.	National Aluminium Company Limited	61.15% (10% domestic issue, 20% ADR issue, 29.15% strategic sale, 2% to employees)
5.	National Building Construction Corporation Limited	74%
6.	National Fertilizers Limited	53% (51% through strategic sale and 2% to employees)
7.	Rashtriya Chemicals and Fertilizers Limited	53% (51% through strategic sale and 2% to employees)
8.	Hindustan Petroleum Corporation Limited	39.01 % (34.01% through strategic sale and 5% to employees)
9.	Engineers India Limited	61% (51% through strategic sale and 10% to employees)
10.	Balmer Lawrie and Company Limited	61.8%
11.	Engineering Projects India Limited	74%
12.	Hindustan Paper Corporation Limited	74%
13.	State Trading Corporation of India Limited	75% (65% through strategic sale and 10% to employees)

Source: www.divest.nic.in

Sale of minority shareholding through Initial Public Offerings (IPO), and Follow on Public Offerings (FPO)

On 27th January, 2005, Government decided, in principle, to list large, profitable PSEs on domestic stock exchanges and to selectively sell a minority stake in listed, profitable PSEs while retaining at least 51% of the shares along with full management control so as not to disturb the Public Sector character of the companies. Government also decided to constitute a National Investment Fund (NIF) into which the realization from sale of minority shareholding of the Government in profitable PSEs would be canalized. NIF is to be maintained outside the Consolidated Fund of India. The income from NIF would be used for the following broad investment objectives:

(a) Investment in social sector projects which promote education, health care and employment and
(b) Capital investment in selected profitable and revivable public sector enterprises that yield adequate returns in order to enlarge their capital base to finance expansion diversification.

On 25th November, 2005 Government decided, in principle, to list large, profitable PSEs on domestic stock exchanges and to selectively sell small portions of equity in listed, profitable PSEs (other than the Navratna). Further, on 6th July, 2006, Government decided to keep all disinvestment decisions and proposals on hold, pending further review.

Thus, the momentum regarding disinvestment gathered during the current Government has definitely slowed down. With the result, the prospect of disinvestments appears to be slowed down in the near future. Ministry of Disinvestment is now just be a department under the Ministry of Finance with Finance Minister and Prime Minister deciding the future policies on disinvesting the PSEs with effect from 27th May, 2004 and was assigned the following work:

(a) All matters relating to disinvestment of Central Government equity from Central Public Sector Undertakings.
(b) Decisions on the recommendations of Disinvestment Commission on the modalities of disinvestment, including restructuring.
(c) Implementation of disinvestment decisions, including appointment of advisors, pricing of shares, and other terms and conditions of disinvestment.
(d) Disinvestment Commission.
(e) Central Public Sector Undertakings for purposes of disinvestment of Government equity only.

ORGANISATIONAL STRUCTURE OF DEPARTMENT OF DISINVESTMENT

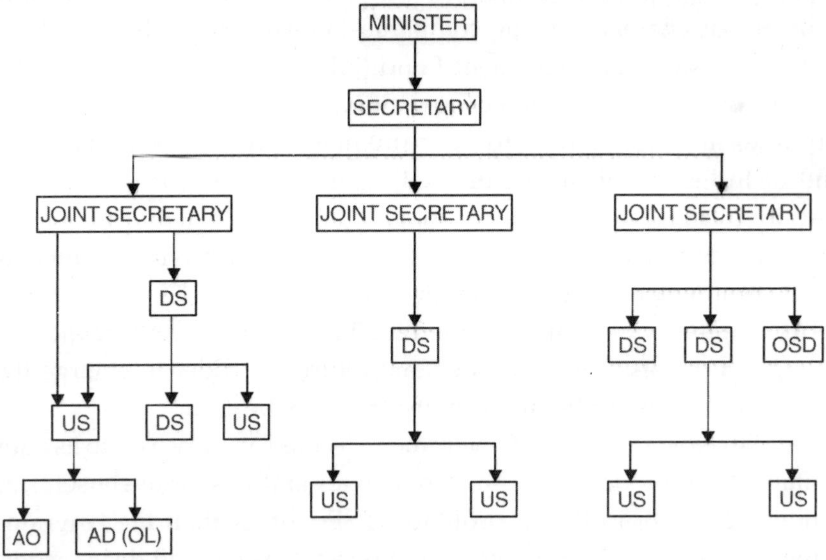

Abbreviations Used: DS: Deputy Secretary, US: Under Secretary, OSD: Officer on Special Duty, AO: Accounts Officer and AD (OL): Assistant Director (Official Language).

Official language policy

The department has a full-fledged Hindi Section for handling all work relating to official language.

E-governance

Personal computers with requisite software have been provided to all officers and personal assistants. Local Area Network (LAN) has been set-up and connectivity provided among all officers. Twenty-four hour internet connectivity is also available to all through NIC. E-mail ID numbers have been issued to all officers who are receiving official communications through it. The officers and staff have been receiving training at NIC from time to time.

The website of the department (www.divest.nic.in) contains data and information (Bilingual) regarding policy, guidelines, procedure, and progress relating to the disinvestment cases. The site is updated on continuous basis. All advertisements when issued in newspapers are simultaneously placed on the website. The publications of the department are also available on the website.

Grievances redressal

The nature of the allocated business of the department does not create much of an interface with the public at large. Still, Joint Secretary in-charge of Administration has been nominated as Director of Public Grievances who ensures quick disposal of public grievances, if any. During the year the department received 28 grievances and all these cases have been resolved. All the grievances were attended to and disposed of promptly.

Vigilance machinery

The initial examination and handling of disinvestment related matters is done at the level of Under Secretary/Deputy Secretary/Director. The Personnel, Administration, Security, Common Services and Vigilance matters are dealt with by a multifunctional service section. The Administration Cell which includes Vigilance is handled by one Joint Secretary. The Deputy Secretary incharge of Administration is also the Chief Vigilance Officer of the Department. During the year no Vigilance or Disciplinary case was pending.

Some of the important initiatives taken by UPA government during the year are given below:

- The disinvestment of Government equity in public sector enterprises will be carried out in accordance with the policy laid down in the National Common Minimum Programme.
- Government has decided, in principle, to list large, profitable Public Sector Enterprises (PSEs) on domestic stock exchanges and to selectively sell a minority stake in listed, profitable PSEs while retaining at least 51% of the shares along with full management control so as not to disturb the public sector character of the companies.
- Government has also decided to constitute a 'National Investment Fund' into which the realization from sale of minority shareholding of the Government in profitable PSEs would be channelised. The fund would be maintained outside the Consolidated Fund of India. The income from the fund would be used for the following broad investment objectives:

  (i) Investment in social sector projects which promote education, health care and employment; and

  (ii) Capital investment in selected profitable and revivable public sector enterprises that yield adequate returns, in order to enlarge their capital base to finance expansion/diversification.

Further, the momentum regarding disinvestment gathered during the UPA Government so far has definitely slowed down. With the result, the prospect of disinvestments appears to be slowed down in the near future.

Expert Comments on Disinvestment Policy of the UPA Government

> "This is the most pig-headed strategy of the UPA government. Sale of assets is possible only when there is a buyer and a buyer will be present when the assets are profitable. Historic trends suggest that the loss-making assets realize a sub-optimal value and the price of loss-making assets do not fetch the bargain price set by the seller (*i.e.*, the government). Thus, the buyers dictate the price of a loss-making asset."—*Jamsheyd Desai, Head of Equity Research, IL & FS*

> "PSEs must be disinvested and the government should not be in the business of doing business."
>
> —*Deena Mehta, Managing Director, Asit C. Mehta*

There is no doubt that the disinvestment today has become a necessary evil. Achieving a GDP growth of seven to eight per cent requires political will to implement disinvestment. Having two economists in the pilot and co-pilot seats, let us hope the coming budget might see the UPA government on a correction course.[4]

NOTES

1. IOC Annual Report, 2000-2001.
2. The Times of India, 17 September, 2000.
3. Here regulation means regulation of the conduct of the business and not the type of growth defeating hassles we have had.
4. Ved, Urvashi. *Capital Market Magazine*, June 7–20, 2004 Edition, p. 10.

REFERENCES

1. Department of Public Enterprises, *Guidelines for Investment of Surplus Funds by PSEs*, DPE-Om No. DPE/4/6/94 Fin., December 14, 1994.

2. *Future Privatizations—A Future History of Privatizations:* 1992–2002, in Economist, Vol. 321, No. 7738, Dec. 21 1991–Jan. 3 1992, pp. 15–18.
3. GOPALKRISHNA, M. *Disinvestment and Restructuring of Public Enterprises in India—Some Reflections,* in The Journal of Institute of Public Enterprises, Vol. 20, No. 3 & 4, October–December 1997.
4. JACOB, C.S. *Disinvestment of PSU Share: Was the Price Right?,* Private Circulation by Department of Public Enterprises, Government of India, 1993.
5. JAFA, V.S. *Liberalization in India: The Road Ahead,* New Century, 2001.
6. KAY, J.A. AND THOMPSON, D.J. *Privatization: A Policy in Search of a Rationale,* in The Economic Journal, Vol. 96, March 1986, pp. 18–32.
7. KHANDAWALA, P.N. *Dynamics of Corporate Regeneration,* RVB Research Papers, Vol. IX, No. 1, June 1989.
8. SINGH, MAMATS. *Department of Disinvestment to Move Fresh Cabinet Note on Maruti sell-off,* in Business Standard, New Delhi, November 3, 2000.
9. SINGH, PARVEEN. *Cabinet Clears Disinvestments in IBP, MMTC, STC,* The Economic Times, October 6, 2000.
10. VITTA, L.N. *Disinvestment Through Disincentives,* in The Economic Times, September 1, 2000.
11. World Bank. *Country Study, India—Recent Economic Developments & Prospects,* World Bank Report, 1995.
12. World Bank. *Economic Developments in India: Achievements and Challenges,* Washington D.C., World Bank, 1995.

Appendix A

DETAILS OF FULL SAMPLE OF 48 PSEs

Sl. No.	*Name of PSEs*	*% Shares disinvested*
1.	Andrew Yule (AY)	9.60
2.	Bharat Earth Movers Limited (BEML)	32.28
3.	Bharat Electronics Limited (BEL)	24.14
4.	Bharat Heavy Electronics Limited (BHEL)	32.28
5.	Bharat Petrochemical Corporation Limited (BPCL)	33.80
6.	Bangargaon Refinery and Petrochemical Limited (BRPL)	24.54
7.	Bharat Aluminium and Locomotive Company (BALCO)	51.00
8.	Cochin Refineries Ltd. (CRL)	6.12
9.	Computer Maintenance Corporation (CMC)	77.00
10.	Container Corporation of India Limited (CONCOR)	36.92
11.	Dredging Corporation of India Limited (DCI)	1.44
12.	Engineers India Limited (EIL)	5.98
13.	Fertilizers and Chemicals (Travancore) Limited (FACT)	1.70
14.	Gas Authority of India Limited (GAIL)	42.66
15.	Hindustan Cables Limited (H Cab L)	1.04
16.	Hindustan Copper Limited (H Cop L)	1.24
17.	Hindustan Machine Tools Limited (HMT)	8.44
18.	Hindustan Photo Films Manufacturing Corp. Limited (HPF)	9.87
19.	Hindustan Organic Chemicals Limited (HOCL)	41.39*
20.	Hindustan Petroleum Corporation Limited (HPCL)	48.94*
21.	Hindustan Teleprinters Limited (HTL)	74.00
22.	Hindustan Zinc Limited (HZL)	76.08
23.	ICI India Limited (ICI)	9.2
24.	Indian Oil Corporation (IOC)	17.85
25.	Indian Telephone Industries Limited (ITI)	22.98
26.	IBP Limited (IBP)	100.00

(*Contd.*)

27.	Indian Petrochemicals Corporation Limited (IPCL)	99.00
28.	Indian Railway Construction Company Limited (IRCON)	0.27
29.	Indian Tourism Development Corporation Limited (ITDC)	100
30.	Jessop and Company Ltd. (Jessop)	72.00
31.	Kudremukh Iron Ore Company Limited (KIOCL)	1.00
32.	Minerals and Metals Trading Corporation Limited (MMTC)	0.67
33.	Maruti Udyog Limited (MUL)	42.7
34.	Mahanagar Telephone Nigam Limited (MTNL)**	43.80
35.	Modern Food Industries (India) Limited (MFIL)	100.00
36.	Madras Refineries Limited (MRL)	16.92
37.	National Fertilizers Limited (NFL)	2.35
38.	National Aluminium Company Limited (NALCO)	12.85
39.	National Thermal Power Corporation (NTPC)	9.25
40.	National Mineral Development Corporation Limited (NMDC)	1.62
41.	Neyveli Lignite Corporation Limited (NLC)	6.01
42.	Oil and Natural Gas Commission (ONGC)	26.37
43.	Paradeep Phosphates Limited (PPL)	74.00
44.	Rashtriya Chemicals and Fertilizers Limited (RCFL)	7.50
45.	Shipping Corporation of India Limited (SCI)	19.88
46.	Steel Authority of India Limited (SAIL)	14.18*
47.	State Trading Corporation (STC)	48.97
48.	Videsh Sanchar Nigam Limitd (VSNL)*	74.00

Source: Up to 1997-98, data was collected from Public Enterprises Survey Vol. I, various years. For later years, figures were obtained from website of Ministry of Disinvestment (www.divest.nic.in)

Note: * Including dilution of Government shareholding by public issue/GDR issues.
** The balance equity is held by state governments/other collaborations.

Appendix B

SUMMARY OF YEARWISE DISINVESTMENT OF PSEs' SHARES TILL DATE

Year	*No. of companies in which equity sold*	*Target receipt for the year (Rs. in crore)*	*Actual receipts (Rs. in crore)*	*Methodology*
1991-92	47 (31 in one tranche and 16 in other)	2,500	3,038	Minority shares sold by auction method in bundles of 'very good', 'good', and 'average' companies.
1992-93	35 (in 3 tranches)	2,500	1,913	Bundling of shares abandoned, Shares sold separately for each company by auction method.
1993-94	–	3,500	0	Equity of 7 companies sold by open auction but proceeds received in 94-95.
1994-95	13	4,000	4,843	Sale through auction method, in which NRIs and other persons legally permitted to buy, hold or sell equity allowed to participate.
1995-96	5	7,000	361	Equities of 4 companies auctioned and Government piggy backed in the IDBI fixed price offering for the 5th company.

(*Contd.*)

1996-97	1	5,000	380	GDR (VSNL) in international market.
1997-98	1	4,800	902	GDR (MTNL) in international market.
1998-99	5	5,000	5,371	GDR (VSNL)/Domestic offerings with the participation of FIIs (CONCOR, GAIL). Cross purchase by 3 Oil sector companies, *i.e.*, GAIL, ONGC & IOC.
1999-00#	4	10,000	1,860	GDR-GAIL, VSNL—domestic issue, BALCO — restructuring, MFIL's strategic sale and others.
2000-01	4	10,000	1,871	Strategic sale of BALCO, LJMC; Takeover — KRL (CRL), CPCL (MRL), BRPL.
2001-02#	9	12,000	5,632	Strategic sale of CMC—51%, HTL—74%, VSNL — 25%, IBP — 33.58%, PPL — 74%, and sale by other modes: ITDC & HCI; surplus reserves: STC and MMTC.
2002-2003	6	12,000	3,348	Strategic sale : HZL — 26%, MFIL — 26%, IPCL — 25% HCI, ITDC, Maruti: control premium from renunciation of rights issue, ESOP, HZL, CMC.

2003-2004	9	13,200	15,547	Maruti— IPO (27.5%), Jessop & Co. Ltd. (Strategic sale— 72%), HZL (Call Option of SP — 18.92%), Public Offers — IPCL (28.95%), CMC (26%), IBP (26%), DRDG (20%), GAIL (10%), ONGC (10%), ICI (9.2%)
2004-2005	3	4,000	2,765	NTPC (IPO) (5.25%), IPCL (5%) to employees and ONGC (0.01%)
2005-2006			1567.60	By sale of shares to Public Sector Financial Institutions and Public Sector Banks on 'Differential Pricing Method'

Source: Department of Disinvestment. *Website:* www.divest.nic.in

Notes: * Total no. of companies in which disinvestment has taken place so far.

Figures (inclusive of amount expected to be realized, control premium, dividend/dividend tax and transfer of surplus cash reserves prior to disinvestment etc.) (Rs. 31 crore taxes from BALCO).

GLOSSARY

Accumulated loss is a formal examination or verification of an organization or individual's accounts or financial situation by a professional.

Acquisition is the process through which one company takes over the controlling interest of another through either the purchase of its shares, or the purchase of its assets. A company that attempts to acquire another company is known as acquiring company. The company which is being solicited by the acquiring company is known as Target Company. Generally, the company that is being acquired typically sees its share price appreciate right after the acquisition takes place. The company doing the buying usually sees its stock price fall.

Advanced SWOT analysis involves developing a two-dimensional matrix and assessing some or all of the strengths, weaknesses, opportunities and threats against external environmental factors or against the key functions of business.

Advertising is undertaken by organizations to attract new customers or retain existing customers. Advertising takes place in a variety of places: on TV, on radio, in the cinema, on the web, in the press. Firms usually have to pay to advertise in any of these media.

After-sales customer service is provided by organizations to support customers who have purchased and are using their products and services. Common examples include repair and maintenance services.

Agency problems is the conflict of interests that may result between the management and shareholders or the creditors (debt holders).

Asset management company is a firm that invests the pooled funds of retail investors in securities in line with the stated investment objectives.

For a stipulated fee, the investment company provides more diversification, liquidity, and professional management service than is normally available to individual investors.

Asset turnover ratio is an overall measure of how effectively assets are used during a period; computed by dividing net sales by average total assets.

Assets are things which companies own, such as buildings and stock.

Bid is an offer/wish/attempt/price at which a buyer has offered to purchase some asset.

Capacity is a measure of performance, and if a system is operating to capacity, it is producing the maximum amount of product over a specified time period.

Capital is money which a company raises to acquire assets and comes from sources such as bank loans, retained profits and shares.

Centralization is the concentration of decision-making responsibility in the hands of managers at the top of an organization.

Claw-back provision means when the concerned institutions subsequently sold these shares to the general public, reasonable fixed percentage of the gain would be transferred to the exchequer.

Common minimum programme is a document outlining the minimum objectives of a coalition government. The document has acquired prominence since coalition governments have become the norm in India.

Creditors are individuals or companies to which a firm owes money.

Customer acquisition is expanding the number of customers for existing products.

Customer diversification is achieved by increasing sales of a new product or service to new customers.

Customer extension is concerned with extending the range of products or services available for a customer to purchase from the organization.

Customer loyalty is the behaviour exhibit when they make frequent repeat purchases of a brand.

Debtors are individuals or other companies which owe firm money.

Decentralization is the dispersal of decision-making responsibility to operational managers.

Differential pricing method is the pricing of an issue where one category is offered shares at a price different from the other category is called differential pricing. It is allowed only if the securities to applicants in the firm allotment category are at a price higher than the price at which the net offer to the public is made. The net offer to the public means the offer made to the Indian public and does not include firm allotments or reservations or promoters' contributions.

Differentiation is serving a broad target market, but by providing a product or service that is different and better due to its added value.

Direct costs are the expenditure on elements that go straight into producing the product or service, e.g., raw materials.

Discounted cash flow method of investment appraisal takes account of returns in later years being worth less than returns in the early years of a project.

Disinvestment means transfer of ownership and/or management of an enterprise from the public sector to private hands. It also means the withdrawal of the state from an industry or sector, partially or fully. In another words, disinvestment stands for opening up of an industry that has been reserved for the public sector to the private sector. Therefore, disinvestment simply is the withdrawal of capital from a public corporation.

Distribution is the method by which goods and services are delivered to customers.

Diversification is using new products to move into a new market, in which the company has not previously operated.

Dividend payments are the share of profits paid out to the shareholders of a business.

Dividend payout ratio is a measure of the percentage of earnings paid out in dividends; computed by dividing cash dividends by the net available income.

Downsizing is when a company reduces its workforce due to the impact of technological changes, changes in government policies or reduced demand of product and services by selling off, closure of some plants, combination of operations performing the same functions, and/or cost cutting of an enterprise when its growth levels are off or reversed.

Efficiency is the ratio of actual output to possible output, usually expressed as a percentage.

Entrepreneurship is the practice of starting new organizations, particularly new businesses by taking personal initiative. In simple words, entrepreneurship is the willingness to take risks involved in starting and managing a business.

Extension strategy is a plan for lengthening the life cycle of a product or service.

External environment is the big wide world in which organizations operate. It encompasses the broad general environment, the competitive environment and the marketplace.

Financial restructuring means changing the capital structure of an organization e.g., through leveraged buy-outs etc. for the purpose of bringing out a company from financial difficulty.

Fiscal deficit is total expenditure including loans minus (revenue receipts + grants + non-debt capital receipts).

Fixed costs do not change directly in relation to the level of productivity, but are paid on a regular basis, e.g., rent and insurance.

Fixed position layouts are used when the product is too big or heavy to move, as in shipbuilding, airplane assembly and oil rig construction. All the operations are carried out on one site around the static product.

Free market occurs where there is little or no regulation of commercial activity by government.

GDP is the total value of goods and services produced by a nation. The total value of all goods and services produced within the boundaries of a particular country in any given year.

GDR is a dollar denominated instrument traded on the stock exchanges in Europe or US or both. Usually they represent a certain number of equity shares. Though GDR is denominated in dollars, the underlying shares are denominated in rupees.

Globalization is a set of processes leading to the integration of economic, cultural, political, and social systems across geographical boundaries.

Hypothesis is a theory or tentative assumption whose validity is yet to be tested by further examination.

Intangible resources include things like brand image and information.

Interest is what stakeholders seek from an organization, e.g., employees have an interest in the wages an organization pays.

Market research is the way by which companies identify who is in the market place, their location, and their needs and wants.

Marketing is the identification and meeting of customer needs and wants.

Market place is where the company's products are sold and can be defined by types of customers and/or location.

Merger occurs when two companies join together into one, with one company surviving and the other company disappearing. The assets and liabilities of the disappearing entity are absorbed into the surviving entity. Generally mergers occur in a consensual setting where executives from the target company help those from the purchaser in a due diligence process to ensure that the deal is beneficial to both companies.

Mixed economy is an 'economy that combines capitalism and socialism'. Certain sectors of the economy are left to private ownership and free market mechanisms, while other sectors have significant government ownership and government planning.

Monetized deficit is increase in net RBI credit to the central government, comprising to the net increase in the holdings of treasury bills of the RBI and its contribution to the market borrowings of the government.

Monopoly is a market situation, in which there is a single supplier of a good, service, or resource that has no close substitutes and in which there is a barrier preventing the entry of new firms into the industry.

Nationalization is the act of taking assets into state ownership. Usually it refers to private assets being nationalized, but sometimes it may be assets owned by other levels of government, such as municipalities.

Nonviable organizations are those whose liquidation value is greater than their value as a going concern, taking into account potential restructuring costs, the 'equilibrium' exchange rate, and interest rates.

Null hypothesis is a very useful tool in testing the significance of difference. In its simplest form the hypothesis asserts that there is no true difference in the sample and the population under consideration.

Opportunities exist in an organisation's external environment and often take the form of new markets or new chances for a firm to sell its products and services.

Organizational restructuring is essential to stay up to date. Managers periodically examine the organizational structure of their company to assure that it maintains to provide an environment for organizational development. Organizations that cannot or don't learn become obsolete.

Plan expenditure is the expenditure of the government which is developmental in nature and is spent on schemes detailed in the central plan. Otherwise any sudden expense or the expense not mentioned in the plan is an example of non-plan expenditure.

Portfolio restructuring means making additions to or disposals from companies' businesses g., through acquisitions or spin-offs and is normally applicable to derivative products. In simple terms, it is decomposition of a portfolio's asset mix by selling off undesired asset types (equities, debt, or cash) or specific securities within that class, while simultaneously buying desired types or securities. For this, often a company is asked to bid on an old portfolio and give an offering of the desired portfolio.

Pricing mechanism is the method through which the market organizes and adjusts itself. Prices determine what is produced, how it's produced and who receives the product. If the market is working correctly, the workings of the price mechanism should result in the most efficient allocation of resources.

Primary data is collected directly from people and organizations via questionnaires or surveys before being analyzed to reach conclusions concerning the issues covered in the questionnaire or survey.

Primary deficit is fiscal deficit less interest payments.

Privatization is the process of selling public enterprises/assets into the private hands e.g., water, power, electricity etc. Usually involves an offer for sale to the general public of its shares.

Product life cycle is one of the marketing tools. The product life cycle can be used to examine the sales and profits a product or service is making, relative to the length of time in the market place.

Productivity means output relative to input. Higher productivity does not mean adding more inputs but using the resources better.

Prospectus is a legal, written document giving details about an offering of securities investment for sale to the public with detailed financial background of the investment.

Public auction is a gathering at a pre-announced public location for buying and selling things by offering them up for bid, taking bids, and then selling the item to the highest bidder. This method works particularly well when there is no doubt that there will be significant interest in the property.

Public interest theory assumes that where private ownership is proficient, public ownership would do equally well and in case of market failure; public enterprises can do better by correcting the misalignment of the public with the objectives of private sector, as it allows the government to achieve distributional objectives.

Public sector enterprise is that part of economic and administrative life that deals with the delivery of goods and services by and for the government, whether national, regional or local/municipal. It comprises the sub-sectors of general government (mainly central, state and local government units together with social security funds imposed and controlled by those units) as well as public corporations, i.e., corporations that are subject to control by government units.

Pull factors attract or pull an organization towards a new location, e.g., the availability of cheap skilled labour.

Push factors result from dissatisfaction with existing locations, hence causing the organization to consider changing location.

Restructuring means the series of processes to reorganize asset structure, financial structure, and corporate governance, helping the survival and the growth of a corporation. Although the extent of corporate restructuring includes a distressed company as a target in a narrow term, it includes an inefficient company as a target in a broader term.

Return on assets measures the return a company generates from its total assets. It is calculated by PBDIT (Profit Before Depreciation and Income Tax) divided by total assets. It is an indicator of profitability of an organization.

Return on equity is the net income expressed as a percentage of average equity. Return on equity is calculated by dividing net earnings by average stockholders' equity. It is calculated by PBDIT/total equity.

Return on sales is a profitability ratio measured by net profit relative to sales. It is also identified as profit margin and indicates profitability and the operational efficiency of the business. A decline in ROS indicates higher levels of expenses or a decline in sales price.

Revenue deficit is the difference between revenue receipts and revenue expenditures.

Securities and Exchange Board of India (SEBI) is a board (autonomous body) created by the Government of India in 1988 and given statutory form in 1992 with the SEBI Act, 1992 with its head office at Mumbai. The board comprises wholetime members and outside members (representing the finance ministry, RBI and experts). Relatively a brief act containing 35 sections, the SEBI Act governs all the stock exchanges and the securities transactions in India.

Takeover is a change in a corporation's controlling interest through either a friendly acquisition or a hostile bid. Hostile takeovers aim to replace the target company's existing management and are usually attempted through a public tender offer. Other takeover methods are unsolicited merger proposals to directors, accumulation of shares in the open market, or proxy fights.

Tangible products are those which customers can see and touch.

Tangible resources are physical resources and include things like machines and money.

Threats are in an organization's external environment and can take the form of e.g., competition or tighter industry regulation.

Upset price is commonly known as the reserve price. It is a pre-established amount, below which the seller is not required to accept the winning bid.

World Trade Organization (WTO) is the global international organization dealing with the rules of trade between nations. WTO deals with the rules of trade between nations at a global or near-global level; it is responsible for negotiating and implementing new trade agreements, and is in charge of policing member countries' adherence to all the WTO agreements, signed by the bulk of the world's trading nations and ratified in their parliaments.

SELECTED BIBLIOGRAPHY

1. Alesina, Alberto, "Macroeconomics and Politics", *NBER Macroeconomics Annual* (Cambridge, Mass.: National Bureau of Economic Research, 1988), pp. 13–52.
2. Annual Reports (2000-2003) of SAIL, BHEL, IOC, ITI, BEL, BEML and NFL.
3. Agrawal, Pradeep, Financial Reforms, Policy Options for Economic Reform, Indian Merchant's Chamber and IGIDR, Bombay 1992, Bardhan, Pranab, *The Political Economy of Development in India* (Oxford: Basil Blackwell, 1984).
4. Bansal, Rahul, Corporate Restructuring: Adopt ESOP, in *The Economic Times,* New Delhi, November 30, 1993.
5. Basant, Rakesh and Morris Sebastian (2000), "Competition Policy in India: Issues for a Globalizing Economy", *Report from Ministry of Industry,* Indian Institute of Management, Ahmedabad.
6. Bhagwati, J. (1998). "India's Economic Reforms: Dismantling the Machine for Going Backwards", Vikalpa, **23 (1):** 5–7.
7. Bhaya, H. (1990), "Management Efficiency in the Private and Public Sectors in India" in J. Heath (ed.), *Public Enterprises at the Crossroads,* London: Routledge.
8. Bishop, M. and J. Kay (1988), "Does Privatisation Work?" *Lessons from UK,* London Business School.
9. Boyd, C.W. (1986), "The Comparative Efficiency of State-owned Enterprise" in A. Negandhi, H. Thomas and K.L.K. Rao (eds.), *Multinational Enterprises and State-owned Enterprises: A New Challenge in International Business,* Greenwich: JAI Press.
10. Cassen and Vijay Joshi (eds.), "India: The Future of Economic Reform" Delhi: Oxford University Press, 1995.

11. Central Finance Commission, (2000). Report of the Eleventh Finance Commission for 2000–05, *Special Supplement No. 3* (2000), Akalanle Publications, Delhi.
12. Central Statistical Organization (various issues). National Accounts Statistics, CSO, New Delhi.
13. Centre for Monitoring the Indian Economy (2000). Infrastructure Statistics Report, CMIE, Mumbai.
14. Dalal, Sucheta, "Why Aren't the Institutions Accountable?" *Times of India*, 6 July 1995.
15. Dalmia, Gaurav, "Reforms and Indian Businessmen", *Economic Times*, 10 November 1993.
16. Dandavate, Madhu, "Patronage to Maruti: Government's Policy of Double—Faced Liberalization", *Indian Express*, 1 December 1993.
17. Gopalakrishna M., Disinvestments and Restructuring of Public Enterprises in India—Some Reflections, in *The Journal of Institute of Public Enterprises*, Vol. 20, No. 3 & 4, 1996, p. 86.
18. Statement on Industrial Policy, 24 July, 1991.
19. Comptroller and Auditor General of India, *Report No. 14* (1993), related to Disinvestment of Government Shareholding in Selected Public Sector Enterprises during 1991-92.
20. Disinvestment: Policy and Procedures, Department of Disinvestment.
21. Disinvestment Policy, Procedures and Progress, Ministry of Disinvestment. Datta-Chaudhuri, Mrinal, "Liberalization without Reform", *Seminar No.* 437 (January 1996), pp. 32–35.
22. Datta-Chaudhuri, Mrinal, "The New Policy", *Seminar* (December 1985), pp. 18–22.
23. Dhar, P.N., "The Political Economy of Development in India", *Indian Economic Review*, Vol. XXII, No. 1 (1987), pp. 1–18.
24. Dixit, A. (1980), "The Role of Investment in Entry Deterrence", *The Economic Journal*, 90 (March): 95–106.
25. Economic Survey (Various Issues).
26. Government of India, Finance Ministry, *Economic Survey* 1994/95 (New Delhi: Government Printing Office, 1995).
27. Government of India, Ministry of Finance, *Economic Survey* 1996/97 (New Delhi, 1997) Government of India, Ministry of Finance, Economic Survey 1994/95 (New Delhi, 1995).
28. Government of India, *National Report on Tax Reform* (New Delhi: Government Printing Office, 1993).

29. Government of India, Office of the Comptroller and Auditor General, *Report on the Disinvestment of Public-Sector Enterprises*, 1991–92 (New Delhi: Government Printing Office, 1993).
30. Joshi, Vijay, and Little, I.M.D. "Macroeconomic Stabilization in India, 1991-93 and beyond", in Robert Cassen and Vijay Joshi (eds.), *India: The Future of Economic Reform* (Delhi: Oxford University Press, 1995).
31. Kohli, Atul, "The Politics of Liberalization in India", *World Development*, Vol. 17, 1989.
32. Mahapatra, L.K. (1999), "Resettlement, Impoverishment and Reconstruction in India", Vikas Publications, New Delhi.
33. Majumdar, S.K. (1995), "Public, Joint and Private Sectors in Indian Industry—Evaluating Relative Performance Differences", *Economic and Political Weekly*, XXX (7-8): M25-32 (18 February).
34. Manor, James, "Tried, then Abandoned: Economic Liberalization in India", *IDS Bulletin*, Vol. 18, No. 4 (1987), pp. 39–44.
35. Monga Kumar Anil, Divesting State Ownership —A Case Study of Haryana, in *The Journal of Institute of Public Enterprises*, Vol. 22, July-September, October-December, 1999.
36. Mukul Akshaya, and Ramachandran Rajesh, Disinvestment will end Reservations, *The Times of India*, New Delhi, January 5, 2001.
37. Ministry of Finance (1993), Report of the Committee on Disinvestment of Shares in Public Sector Enterprises.
38. Nagaraj, R. (1984), "Subcontracting in Indian Industries: Analysis, Evidence and Issues", *Economic and Political Weekly*, Vol. 19, Nos. 31, 32 and 33, pp. 1435–53.
39. Naib, S. (2002), "Ownership—Does it Matter", *Productivity*, **43(2):** 303–313.
40. OECD (2001), "Recent Privatization Trends", *Financial Market Trends*, **79:** 43–65 (June issue).
41. Pryke, R. (1982), "The Comparative Performance of Public and Private Enterprise", *Fiscal Studies*, **3(2):** 68–81.
42. Public Enterprises Survey (Various Issues).
43. Reserve Bank of India, Bulletin, Supplement: "Finances of State Governments—1997-98" (February 1998).
44. Reserve Bank of India, Bulletin, Supplement: "Finances of State Governments—1996-97" (February 1997).
45. Reserve Bank of India, Report on Currency and Finance, 1992 (New Delhi, 1992).

46. Sankar, T.L. and Reddy, Y.V. (1989), "Privatization: Diversification of Ownership of Public Enterprises", Hyderabad: Institute of Public Enterprises and Booklinks Corporation.
47. Singh, Gurbir, "Who Needs an Exit Policy Anyway?" *Economic and Political Weekly*, June 1995, pp. 1359–60.
48. Sharma, A.K., Inviting Public Equity in Government Companies: The State Corporations Revisited, *Lok Udyog*, Vol. 19, No. 4, July 1985, pp. 35–47.
49. Urban Finance (1998), "Urban Infrastructure Finance: Need for a Change in Strategy", Vol. 1, No. 3.
50. World Bank, Country Operations, Industry and Finance Division, Country Department I, South Asia Region, India: Country Economic Memorandum, "Five Years of Stabilization and Reform: The Challenges Ahead", August, 1996.
51. World Bank, Country Operations, Industry and Finance Division, India Country Department, South Asia Region, India: Recent Economic Developments and Prospects (May 27, 1994).

INDEX